Doing Doctoral Research at a Distance

Emerging from personal experience and empirical research, *Doing Doctoral Research at a Distance* is a key companion text for doctoral students from a range of research fields and geographical contexts who are undertaking off-campus, hybrid, and remote pathways.

Offering guidance about the entire off-campus doctoral journey, the book introduces contexts of distance study; key information to get off to a flying start; organising time, space, and plans to get work done; juggling employment, family, and other commitments alongside distance study; doctoral identity and wellbeing; working with doctoral supervisors at a distance; accessing research culture at a distance; and managing the bumps along the road of the distance doctorate. Written for doctoral researchers, this book offers strategies to help those working at a distance to flourish.

This book is ideally suited for those contemplating distance study, distance doctoral students who are starting their off-campus journey, and supervisors and others who are working with distance doctoral researchers.

Katrina McChesney is a Senior Lecturer in Education at the University of Waikato in New Zealand.

James Burford is an Associate Professor of Global Education and International Development in the Department of Education Studies at the University of Warwick, UK.

Liezel Frick is a Professor of Education in the Department of Curriculum Studies and vice-dean for research and postgraduate studies at the Faculty of Education at Stellenbosch University, South Africa.

Tseen Khoo is Co-Founder of The Research Whisperer and a Senior Lecturer in Research Education and Development at La Trobe University, Australia.

Insider Guides to Success in Academia

Series Editors: Helen Kara, Independent Researcher, UK and **Pat Thomson**, The University of Nottingham, UK.

The *Insider Guides to Success in Academia* series addresses topics too small for a full-length book on their own, but too big to cover in a single chapter or article. These topics have often been the stuff of discussions on social media, or of questions in our workshops. We designed this series to answer these questions and to provide practical support for doctoral and early career researchers. It is geared to concerns that many people experience. Readers will find these books to be companions who provide advice and help to make sense of everyday life in the contemporary university.

We have therefore:

(1) invited scholars with deep and specific expertise to write. Our writers use their research and professional experience to provide well-grounded strategies to particular situations.

(2) asked writers to collaborate. Most of the books are produced by writers who live in different countries, or work in different disciplines, or both. While it is difficult for any book to cover all the diverse contexts in which potential readers live and work, the different perspectives and contexts of writers goes some way to address this problem.

We understand that the use of the term 'academia' might be read as meaning the university, but we take a broader view. Pat does indeed work in a university, but spent a long time working outside of one. Helen is an independent researcher and sometimes works with universities. Both of us understand academic—or scholarly—work as now being conducted in a range of sites, from museums and the public sector to industry research and development laboratories. Academic work is also often undertaken by networks which bring together scholars in various locations. All of our writers understand that this is the case, and use the term 'academic' in this wider sense.

These books are pocket sized so that they can be carried around and visited again and again. Most of the books have a mix of examples, stories and exercises as well as explanation and advice. They are written in a collegial tone, and from a position of care as well as knowledge.

Together with our writers, we hope that each book in the series can make a positive contribution to the work and life of readers, so that you too can become insiders in scholarship.

Helen Kara, PhD FAcSS,
independent researcher
https://helenkara.com/
@DrHelenKara (Twitter/Insta)

Pat Thomson PhD PSM FAcSS FRSA
Professor of Education, The University of Nottingham
https://patthomson.net
@ThomsonPat

For a full list of books in the series please go to: www.routledge.com/Insider-Guides-to-Success-in-Academia/book-series/IGSA

Related titles in the Series include:

Thriving in Part-Time Doctoral Study
Integrating Work, Life and Research
Jon Rainford and Kay Guccione

Navigating Your International Doctoral Experience (and Beyond)
Dely Lazarte Elliot

Planning and Passing your PhD Defence
A Global Toolbox for Success
Olga Degtyareva and Eva O.L. Lantsoght

"This text reads like a warm conversation with a friend who is taking you on a tour of a foreign town. As the friend highlights what you can expect, you also get loads of helpful, practical advice to guide you on your journey. I especially liked that the book is peppered with quotes from students all over the world who are themselves doing their doctorate from a distance."

Professor Sioux McKenna, *Director of the Centre for Postgraduate Studies, Rhodes University, South Africa*

"This book is useful for all doctoral students as no one is fully 'present' on campus anymore. All of us are dealing with a pandemic-altered world where hybrid and remote ways of work are the new normal. This book is solidly grounded in the research around doctoral success and will help you navigate myriad practical, social and emotional problems... some of which you have no idea about yet!"

Professor Inger Mewburn *(AKA The Thesis Whisperer), Director of Researcher Development, Australian National University*

Doing Doctoral Research at a Distance

Flourishing in Off-Campus, Hybrid, and Remote Pathways

Katrina McChesney, James Burford, Liezel Frick, and Tseen Khoo

Routledge
Taylor & Francis Group

LONDON AND NEW YORK

Designed cover image: Getty Images

First published 2024
by Routledge
4 Park Square, Milton Park, Abingdon, Oxon OX14 4RN

and by Routledge
605 Third Avenue, New York, NY 10158

Routledge is an imprint of the Taylor & Francis Group, an informa business

© 2024 Katrina McChesney, James Burford, Liezel Frick, and Tseen Khoo

The right of Katrina McChesney, James Burford, Liezel Frick, and Tseen Khoo to be identified as authors of this work has been asserted in accordance with sections 77 and 78 of the Copyright, Designs and Patents Act 1988.

British Library Cataloguing-in-Publication Data
A catalogue record for this book is available from the British Library

ISBN: 978-1-032-36846-7 (hbk)
ISBN: 978-1-032-36847-4 (pbk)
ISBN: 978-1-003-33408-8 (ebk)

DOI: 10.4324/9781003334088

Typeset in Helvetica
by Newgen Publishing UK

Contents

Acknowledgements

It has been a privilege for us to prepare this book and to know that it is forming part of such an excellent and insightful series (the *Insider Guides to Success in Academia*). We are grateful to series editors Pat Thomson and Helen Kara as well as the wider Routledge team for this opportunity and for their input.

Sincere thanks to our colleagues, students, and friends who reviewed drafts of part or all of this book: Dr Brent Abrahams, Mary Eppolite, Dr Jeanette Fyffe, Dr Laura Gurney, Dr Genine Hook, Michelle Marston, Hoana McMillan, Jo McMillan-Chabot, Emma Passey, Clarissa Robertson, Dr Nompilo Tshuma, Andrew Ty, and Thornchanok Uerpairojkit. Thank you to Emma Jones, who spent a summer working with our research data and the doctoral education literature, and to the University of Waikato for funding Emma's involvement. We also thank the anonymous reviewers and the *Doctoral Research by Distance* Facebook group for their feedback, and our respective family, friends, and colleagues for thinking it was pretty cool that we were writing this book.

Finally, our wholehearted appreciation, admiration, and encouragement to the 521 distance doctoral researchers and graduates around the world who completed our research survey in 2022. Your stories moved us, reaffirmed the importance of this work, and helped make this book what it is. Thank you all.

1 Introduction

People in many contexts and circumstances undertake doctoral research. Some "go to work" on their doctorate every weekday, leaving home to work on campus. These doctoral researchers[1] likely have relatively ready access to doctoral student peers; to their supervisors; to purpose-built workspaces such as offices, laboratories, studios, or libraries; and to the community, training, events, and opportunities available on campus. On-campus doctoral researchers are easily visible to the institution and may dominate unconscious assumptions about *who*, *where*, and *how* doctoral researchers are.

But what about everybody else?

This book is written precisely for those researchers who may be left out of dominant imaginings of the doctoral student: those who are located far away from their enrolling institutions, and those who live close enough that they could get to campus but choose (or need) to work elsewhere some or all of the time. Those who leave their homes and communities to undertake doctoral research internationally, perhaps visiting another institution for a portion of their enrolment or conducting fieldwork abroad. Those who are formally enrolled in distance,

DOI: 10.4324/9781003334088-1

online, or hybrid programmes, and those who are forging their own path. Those who choose off-campus study, and those for whom distance is the best or only option due to caring or professional responsibilities, health or mobility challenges, financial pressures, lockdowns, deployments, secondments, incarceration, or maybe even space travel!

Across this book, we demonstrate that doctoral research doesn't have to mean working on campus but can be tailored to suit your context, circumstances, and preferred ways of working. Off-campus and hybrid modes can sometimes seem like anomalies, deviations from what "should" be happening, or not-quite-as-good alternatives, but we resist these assumptions. Instead, this book explores and celebrates the richness of off-campus doctoral journeys.

What is doctoral research by "distance" today, and why think about it?

The title of this book hints at the complexity of understanding what doctoral research by "distance" might mean. We included additional words in the book's subtitle—*off-campus, hybrid, and remote pathways*—to expand what the word "distance" might conjure up in readers' minds. This clarification, however, risks reducing distance modes of study to a series of discrete categories that can miss the uniqueness and fluidity of many doctoral researchers' experiences. If you're coming to this book and wondering whether your own doctoral experience "counts" as distance and whether this book will be relevant to you, we hope you find yourself represented in what follows.

An extremely brief history of distance [doctoral] education

Distance learning itself dates back to the 1700s (Harting & Erthal, 2005). Since its beginnings, distance education has been informed by social justice concerns:

> First-generation distance educators felt it was important to offer educational opportunities to those without easy access to education institutions. These groups often included women and working class people, since neither group was well served by formal education institutions. (Anderson & Simpson, 2012, p. 3)

Distance education at all levels has traditionally been a very isolated, individual endeavour. Distance students have often been "out of sight, out of mind" compared to those on campus and had limited opportunities to interact with peers or to engage in social learning. This has perhaps been particularly true of distance doctoral education: while distance undergraduate or taught postgraduate programmes have increasingly incorporated opportunities for students to work in cohorts and interact online as a community of peers, these elements have been less commonly included in institutions' provision for off-campus doctoral students.

The twenty-first century has seen massive shifts in what distance education can look like. As digital technologies have emerged and advanced, distance education has become increasingly multimodal and diverse. Different vocabulary has come in and out of favour as higher education institutions have explored online learning, eLearning, technology-enhanced learning, artificial intelligence, blended learning, flipped learning, MOOCs (massive open online courses), and more (Fawns, 2019). Social media has also played an increasing role, offering new opportunities for doctoral researchers to find community, support, and professional learning beyond what is available through their enrolling institutions (Sheldon & Sheppard, 2022).

At the same time, however, these digital advances have sharpened the divide between those with and without access to digital resources. Those in the Global South may be confronted with challenges and resource constraints around things that those in Global North settings may simply take for granted. Imagine doctoral students based in rural areas having to travel for hours to bigger towns beyond their villages to simply get access to electricity to recharge their computers, never mind getting connectivity. Doctoral students affected by war, climate change, or other global events may also suddenly find themselves without access to what many would consider the basic infrastructure needed for managing off-campus study.

Most recently, in the post-COVID environment, the distinction between on-campus and distance doctoral researchers has blurred. We suggest that most—but not all—doctoral researchers today will engage in a combination of on- and off-campus modes, driven by their context and circumstances. It has therefore never been so important to consider the experiences and needs of doctoral students located off-campus.

"Distance" doctoral education today

All these developments mean that traditional understandings of "distance education" no longer capture the complexity, flexibility, and diversity of what it may mean to engage in doctoral education away from campus. Where might doctoral research projects take place in our ultra-connected, flexible, twenty-first-century world? How might the spatial features of undertaking a distance doctorate change over the duration of the degree? What rewards, opportunities, challenges, barriers, and strategies arise when doctoral researchers inhabit this diverse range of spaces and places?

As an intuitive, accessible shorthand, we do use the word "distance" in the title of this book, and as our primary descriptor of the audience we are writing for. We still think the origin of the word distance—from the Latin *distare*, literally meaning "standing apart"—captures the fundamental separation or space between doctoral researchers and the physical place of their institutions.

We want to be clear, though, that we're using the term "distance" in flexible, evolving ways that reflect our contemporary context. We don't intend this wording to just signal those who are officially enrolled as "distance", "remote", or "online" learners. We don't restrict our focus just to those who are a large geographic distance away from their institution or to those who are otherwise prevented from getting to campus. Rather, when we write to and about "distance" doctoral researchers, we are really thinking about *anyone who completes part or all of their doctoral work away from the physical site of their institutional campus, by choice or necessity*. This is a very broad group indeed, and one that we expect will continue to grow.

Why we are writing this book

Undertaking doctoral research is a significant undertaking for anyone. It necessitates tremendous identity and skill development requiring guidance from established researchers and the development of academic judgement. Many doctoral researchers experience tensions as they navigate being emerging experts in their fields of study while being novices in the world of research. This is a complex situation for any doctoral researcher, but there are unique considerations for those working at a distance.

Distance doctoral researchers may have reduced access to supervisory input, support services, training and development, networking opportunities, material resources or infrastructure, opportunities to perform new scholarly identities, and the wider institutional climate than their on-campus peers (Nasiri & Mafakheri, 2015; Wisker et al., 2021). All these resources and opportunities, however, are crucially important for the formation of any doctoral researcher! In an age of technology and innovation, it's important to empower distance doctoral researchers to pursue these things where possible. It is also important to challenge supervisors and other institutional players to ensure that those researching at a distance have equitable access and are not left solely responsible for making their modes of study "work".

As a team of authors, our personal experiences shaped our interest in doctoral research by distance and brought us together to write this book. Our experiences have also given us unique perspectives on distance doctoral study and those who undertake it. Two of us completed our own doctoral research by distance, and we share our stories here.

Katrina's distance doctoral story

The first time I set foot on "my" university campus was the day I graduated with my PhD. I had been working in Abu Dhabi when I enrolled in an MPhil (research Masters) through a university from Australia that offered fee-free research programmes for New Zealand citizens. I later converted my enrolment to a PhD, extending the scope and scale of my project. I worked on my PhD for five years part-time, interrupted by around a year's leave in the middle. Alongside my doctorate, I maintained full-time employment for the first three years and part-time employment thereafter; lived in six different homes across two hemispheres; navigated moving home from Abu Dhabi to New Zealand; and had my first baby.

I had one full-time supervisor, Jill, with me throughout my doctoral journey. We met in-person three times during my enrolment: twice when she visited Abu Dhabi on behalf of the university (which ran "nodes" of students in different international contexts) and once when university funding allowed me to present at a conference in Australia. When I got really, really stuck in the late stages of writing up, Jill and I met online once or twice via Skype—in fact, I was the first student she had ever Skyped!—but apart from that, all of my supervision took the form of written feed-back on drafts.

Jill's input was wonderful—and thank goodness, as it was also all I got. The university provided no real support for distance doctoral researchers at that time other than the library's help with scanning and emailing through occasional book chapters. However, thanks to frustratingly frequent emails promoting fabulous-looking workshops, networking, and other events for students located on campus, I was well aware of what I and other distance peers were missing out on. I came away from my PhD with a niggling sense that "somebody should do something to support distance doctoral students"—which, over time, became the genesis for this book and our team's wider work in this area.

Jamie's distance doctoral story

Dunedin (or Ōtepoti) and Auckland (or Tāmaki Makaurau) are at the opposite ends of New Zealand. Approximately 1430 kms and the choppy waters of the Cook Strait separate these cities, and it takes around 2 hours to fly between the two. I applied for doctoral study at the University of Auckland while living in Dunedin. In one of my earliest emails with my prospective supervisors, I gingerly asked where I could base myself. I laid out my situation: I could move to Auckland or stay where I was, where I had a partner, friends, a relevant university-based job, stability, and a lower cost of living. I clicked "send" hoping that the email wouldn't signal that I was an unserious applicant.

The next day I received a reply from one of my future supervisors. She said it was my decision and that she was happy to supervise me from wherever I was. So, that was that. I registered for my institution's "flexible service" for distance students, which meant that library books could be sent to me by post and that wonderful librarians would scan any individual chapters I needed. I would fly up to Auckland semi-regularly for events, but much of my contact with my supervisors and other students was via Skype. Both of my supervisors—Louisa and Barbara—had fantastic groups of students. Louisa's students created an online Facebook group to keep in touch, which was a total lifeline, and we would sometimes catch up for dinner if I was in town. Alongside regular supervision meetings, Barbara ran a group for all her supervisees, which I beamed into from wherever I was.

While I started my distance journey in Dunedin, a whole lot of life can happen during a PhD. Toward the end of the first year, I moved to Christchurch or Ōtautahi to care for my mother, who was seriously ill at the time. This time was characterised by periods of leave and part-time study. Next, I followed a partner to Bangkok, when he got a job and I secured a visiting researcher role and then later a full-time position at a university there. Overall, I thrived via distance study. I felt empowered, connected, and well supported, and I was able to do things that mattered to me like caring for my Mum as well as my PhD.

The team and our shared positioning

The other two members of our team are Liezel Frick and Tseen Khoo. Liezel works at Stellenbosch University in South Africa and works with supervisors and research students across the African continent. She brings rich experience with doctoral education in the Global North and Global South and strong commitments to social justice and accessibility in doctoral education. Tseen is based at La Trobe University in Australia, an institution that has multiple metropolitan and regional campuses. In her role as a researcher developer, Tseen actively supports many postgraduate and early career scholars who are at a distance from the metro campuses. Adding Katrina and Jamie's experiences across New Zealand, Abu Dhabi, Thailand, and the UK, our team is connected to a range of international contexts and student experiences.

All four of us work directly with distance doctoral researchers. We also research higher education with different interests including doctoral and early career researchers' lived experiences, academic conferences, doctoral education admissions, doctoral creativity and originality, trauma and inclusion in doctoral education, supervision, and more. Tseen co-runs the popular *Research Whisperer* blog,[2] Jamie the *Conference Inference* blog,[3] and Katrina *Ipu Kererū*, the blog of the New Zealand Association for Research in Education.[4] Together, we also host the *Doctoral Research by Distance* Facebook group[5] to connect and support a diverse group of distance doctoral researchers.

As a team, we have also researched the experiences of students undertaking doctoral research by distance. Our 2022 online survey captured over 520 responses from doctoral researchers in 42 countries who shared their circumstances, motivations, challenges, experiences, and more. Our participants' voices feed directly into this book, with quotes from survey participants appearing throughout the manuscript. We are grateful to all those who took time to complete our survey; this book is part of our effort to give back to this community.

Our stance in relation to doctoral research at a distance is as follows:

- *We are committed to equity, diversity, and inclusion in higher education*, and we are interested in how these aspirations can be achieved in relation to distance doctoral researchers. We know that distance pathways can be particularly important for minoritised students. We believe that institutions and supervisors have responsibilities to support distance doctoral researchers well.
- *We hold a strengths-based view of distance doctoral education*. We resist the notion that distance doctoral

education is inevitably "second best" compared to on-campus study. Instead, we see distance as a valid pathway with its own richness and affordances. For example, distance doctoral researchers may have particular opportunities to develop confidence, independence, alternative networks, and advocacy skills.

- *We recognise that distance doctoral education is complex, messy, and takes many forms in many contexts.* We don't seek to offer one-size-fits-all prescriptions for distance doctoral researchers, programmes, supervisors, or institutions. Instead, we hope to highlight possibilities, open up space for further thought, and cast a vision of what could be.
- *We recognise that distance doctoral researchers are an extremely diverse group.* We bring an intersectional lens (Crenshaw, 1991) to our thinking. We acknowledge that axes of inequality affect distance doctoral researchers' opportunities, experiences, and outcomes.
- Finally, *we believe that individual doctoral researchers, supervisors, support staff, and institutions all have agency in this space.* The ways things have been done in the past do not have to continue unexamined. The paths others have forged are not the only paths we may take. We all have some level of agency in making distance doctoral education positive and fulfilling for ourselves, those who may come after us, or those we supervise or support.

The purpose of this book

There is a wealth of advice literature available to support doctoral researchers. Books, blogs, websites, and podcasts address topics common to the doctoral experience. The wider series this book is in, the *Insider Guides to*

Success in Academia, has many excellent titles which can help those engaged in doctoral research via any mode.

While distance sometimes "pops up" in existing advice, however, to date there has been limited guidance specifically focused on the uniqueness of *distance* doctoral journeys. This is a significant omission—how do you become a researcher while studying away from campus, where so much of the action happens? What might it be like to be a doctoral researcher working across spaces and places that differ from those of your supervisor(s) and institution? What can help current and prospective distance doctoral researchers enjoy the richness of their doctoral journey? And what could supervisors, institutions, and other key support teams do to support distance doctoral journeys?

This book centres the experiences of doctoral researchers studying partly or fully off-campus. We have engaged with the research literature on both doctoral and distance doctoral study, but this is not a standard academic text. Instead, the book is conversational and practical, offering strategies and insights to make your doctoral research experience the best it can be. As authors, we advocate for you: your choices, your circumstances, and your expectation to enjoy an accessible and fulfilling pathway through doctoral education. We want to support you to make the most of your experiences while simultaneously challenging and equipping those around you—including your supervisors, graduate research school staff, student support staff, institutional policy makers—to recognise and support off-campus students well.

STUDENT VOICE: "I just love learning and thinking. Doing my doctorate by distance and part time allows time and space for ideas to percolate beautifully."

What this book offers

This book is primarily a resource for current and prospective doctoral researchers conducting some or all of their research by distance. You are a broad and diverse audience, spanning disciplines, geographic contexts, socioeconomic and cultural backgrounds, ages, genders, sexualities, career trajectories, academic backgrounds, motivations, research aspirations, and more.

Because the book is written with all of this rich diversity in mind, you will not find instant recipes for "successful" distance doctoral research. What works will vary depending on your individual contexts. However, there are certainly some common issues and things that are important for distance (and all) doctoral researchers to consider, and across this book you will find many examples, real-world accounts, suggestions, and tools to think with. We invite you to consider these possibilities with a sense of openness and agency, reflecting on how you could shape your own distance doctoral journey. To facilitate this, we have included a number of practical exercises designed to help you link the book's content to your individual situation.

As you read, you may feel that some of what we discuss would also apply to on-campus doctoral researchers. We argue that there are important distance conversations to have across a range of what might seem like more generic doctoral steps. Thus, where we have included some general information, we have followed this with specific consideration of distance-related aspects. Finally, we do sometimes draw on research about doctoral education and/or doctoral supervision in general, partly for the reasons above and partly because of the limited research available specifically on doctoral research by distance.

One thing this book *doesn't* seek to do is cater specifically for the needs and experiences of international doctoral students. While these students are distant from their countries of origin, they tend to be enrolled as on-campus students in their new location. This group is equally as important as off-campus students, and we refer international student readers (and others interested in thinking about this group's experiences and needs) to Dely Lazarte Elliot's (2023) excellent book in this same series, entitled *Navigating your International Doctoral Experience (and Beyond)*.

STUDENT VOICE: "[Distance doctoral research means] I can live my life and still invest as much time as I want into my PhD. It makes my life so flexible as I can log on and work when I have time. It means I am there when my kids need me, but I also get to do what I love (my research)."

How to read this book

If you are new to doctoral research, new to off-campus modes, or feeling somewhat lost in your distance doctoral journey, then we recommend you read right through this book. You may not know what you don't know, or what you need to consider—so reading everything (which you can probably do in just one day!) will help you think broadly around your distance doctoral experience. If you have specific areas of need or interest, you can of course dip in and out of specific sections and chapters.

You can read this book alone, and indeed this is how many doctoral researchers do most of their reading, but we invite you to consider whether you might read this book with someone else. Discussing the book with other distance doctoral researchers may be useful, as would sharing its insights and your reflections with friends, partners, parents, or colleagues who want to support you. This book is designed to be accessible and may help these wonderful allies to better understand the journey you are on and the things that could help you flourish. Is your supervisor one of those precious people who is open to new ideas as they support you? If so, you might share this book with them!

We hope that supervisors, graduate research school staff, student support staff, and institutional policy makers will also read this book. We have deliberately not written this book *to* or *for* these audiences because we wish to centre the experiences and needs of distance doctoral researchers. However, reading the book should offer a wide range of insights and new perspectives for those who support distance doctoral researchers. We hope that such readers will take up the challenges offered in this book and talk more with the distance doctoral researchers at their institution about their specific needs, experiences, and ideas.

Overview of the book

This book loosely follows the chronology of a doctoral journey. Having established key foundations in this introductory chapter, the next four chapters explore *what it may be like to be a distance doctoral researcher*. Chapter 2 focuses on the initial decision to study via distance and suggests ways you can get off to a "flying start". Chapter 3 examines the "outer work" of organising life, time, and space for distance doctoral research, and Chapter 4 complements this by zooming in on the "juggling work" of family or care responsibilities, paid work, and other commitments. Chapter 5 explores internal aspects of the distance doctoral research experience (including identity, imposter feelings, perfectionism, belonging, and well-being), considering how off-campus students may experience and navigate these domains.

Chapter 6 focuses on the supervision relationship — which is central to how learning happens for doctoral researchers — and how to make this relationship work well via distance. Chapter 7 zooms out to consider how you can access research culture, learning, and support communities when you are not based primarily on campus, and why looking beyond just your supervisors' input is so important. Chapter 8 then considers the "bumps in the road" that may happen over the course of a project that takes multiple years of your life! Changes and challenges in your family life, work, health, location, supervisor(s) and supporters, and mode of study are all considered here, as is the big change at the end of the doctorate as you emerge, wrestle with the gap suddenly left in your weeks and your mind, and face the big question: "What next?"

Finally, in Chapter 9, we bring together key messages from the book to again affirm the importance, validity, and richness of distance doctoral research and the diversity of those who undertake these pathways.

Activity: Owning your distance doctoral experience

Across this book we invite you to feel a sense of agency around your distance doctoral journey. In a notebook, a social media thread (tagging #DistanceDoctorates), a blog post, or a digital document, write down your own responses to these prompts. Alternatively, have a friend or family member ask you to respond aloud to each prompt.

- For me, doctoral research by "distance" looks like ...
- I choose to engage in doctoral research via "distance" because ...
- Things that are great about my distance journey/situation are ...
- People, places, practices, and things that I find helpful on my distance doctoral journey are ...
- The kind of distance doctoral researcher I want to be is ...
- For me, a great distance doctoral experience would mean ...
- Ways that I can actively shape my distance doctoral journey include ...
- A practical step I can take today to nurture or enhance my distance doctoral experience is ...

STUDENT VOICE: "[Being a distance doctoral student] forced me to get good at virtual collaboration, working remotely with teams, time management, being a good 'digital citizen' and shameless self-promotion: all skills which became really valuable during COVID19 lockdowns when everyone started working from home."

Notes

1 Throughout this book, we deliberately move between referring to "doctoral students" and "doctoral researchers", recognising that the doctoral journey is full of shifting identities. We discuss this

complexity in Chapter 5. We deliberately *don't* talk about "doctoral candidates" because in some contexts, this term signals a specific portion of the doctorate only.

2 https://researchwhisperer.org/
3 https://conferenceinference.wordpress.com/
4 https://nzareblog.wordpress.com/
5 www.facebook.com/groups/doctoralresearchbydistance/

References

Anderson, B., & Simpson, M. (2012). History and heritage in open, flexible, and distance education. *Journal of Open, Flexible and Distance Learning*, *16*(2), 1–10. https://jofdl.nz/index.php/JOFDL/article/view/56

Crenshaw, K. (1991). Mapping the margins: Intersectionality, identity politics, and violence against women of color. *Stanford Law Review*, *43*(6), 1241–1299.

Elliot, D. L. (2023). *Navigating your international doctoral experience (and beyond!)*. Routledge.

Fawns, T. (2019). Postdigital education in design and practice. *Postdigital Science and Education*, *1*(1), 132–145. https://doi.org/10.1007/s42438-018-0021-8

Harting, K., & Erthal, M. (2005). History of distance learning. *Information Technology, Learning, and Performance Journal*, *23*(1), 35–44.

Nasiri, F., & Mafakheri, F. (2015). Postgraduate research supervision at a distance: A review of challenges and strategies. *Studies in Higher Education*, *40*(10), 1962–1969. https://doi.org/10.1080/03075079.2014.914906

Sheldon, J., & Sheppard, V. (2022). *Online communities for doctoral researchers and their supervisors: Building engagement with social media*. Routledge.

Wisker, G., McGinn, M. K., Bengtsen, S. S. E., Lokhtina, I., He, F., Cornér, S., Leshem, S., Inouye, K., & Löfström, E. (2021). Remote doctoral supervision experiences: Challenges and affordances. *Innovations in Education and Teaching International*, *58*(6), 612–623. https://doi.org/10.1080/14703297.2021.1991427

2 Beginning work

Deciding to study at a distance and getting off to a flying start

The decision to undertake doctoral study is a big call for any student. It involves committing years of time and effort to a specific research project, advancing both a field of knowledge and your own development as a researcher. As doctoral education enthusiasts, we believe that this can be an amazing thing to do! Doctoral study affords a rare opportunity to spend years in adult life dedicated to your own learning and personal growth while developing knowledge that can contribute to the communities we serve. Equally, we are aware that doing a doctorate can be disruptive, involving unpredictable identity transformations (see Chapter 5) and profound reconfigurations in how you think and what you spend time doing (see Chapter 3).

This chapter canvasses key considerations for new (including prospective and early-stage) doctoral researchers setting out on the distance doctoral journey. It may also be a valuable resource for mentors who are helping new doctoral researchers to make sense of the beginning steps. The chapter covers three key areas: (i) exploring the reasons for choosing to enrol in a doctorate and for doing this at a distance; (ii) locating a university and supervisor(s) with distance study in mind; and (iii)

DOI: 10.4324/9781003334088-2

strategies for starting well in the early days of the doctoral journey.

Why doctoral research, and why by distance?

> **STUDENT VOICE:** "I literally couldn't have done a doctorate if I had to go into campus every day. Travel costs would be impossible on my scholarship stipend. The alternative (moving nearer to campus) isn't possible because I have a kid at a specialist school."

It might seem that choosing to enrol in doctoral study is not a decision that anyone would take lightly. However, there are a raft of reasons why people take this step, ranging from the wholesome and sensible to the random and tangled-up-in-things. Jamie (author) has heard countless students say that they drifted into doctoral study. Katrina (author), too, did her doctorate "by accident." Some students may be enticed by the promise of scholarship funding, a bit of flattery from a professor, and/or a lack of viable job options after a Master's degree. Family dynamics can play a role: doctoral aspirations may resonate with a middle child who felt overlooked, an older woman who has new space for her own interests once her children have grown up, or a queer child whose identity has become intertwined with ideas of high academic achievement. Jamie has also met folks who embarked on a doctoral programme out of spite, perhaps determined to prove to someone else that they had what it takes. In the survey we conducted with over 500 distance doctoral students, the top five reasons students gave for wanting to undertake a doctorate were: their love and enjoyment of learning, a desire to improve their personal life and future opportunities, a desire to make a difference to their community or society, a desire to become a researcher, and a desire to increase their skills and knowledge for work.

Let us quickly say: this is a judgement free zone! Whatever reason for becoming a "Dr" burns inside you has clearly been motivating enough to bring you to this point in your journey. Nonetheless, it is still sensible to set off with some introspection. Gaining clarity about what you want from your doctoral experience gives you the opportunity to design the kind of journey that will allow you to meet your aspirations. So, what does enrolling in a doctorate mean for you? Do you want to learn, create, test yourself, give back, travel overseas, retreat into a library, cure cancer, stand up for your community, prepare yourself for a future job, kill some time, and/or figure out who you are? Whatever the *why* is for you, try your best to locate it. If you have multiple *why*s, do some "rise to the top" as being the most important drivers for your decision to undertake a doctorate? Your *why* might shift along the thesis[1] journey, and that's okay too.

Next, let's think about a related question: why (your particular configuration of) *distance* doctoral study? Location is one of the most common reasons for off-campus doctoral research. People who live in geographically remote or rural settings and/or near institutions that do not offer doctoral degrees face a barrier of proximity that makes it difficult to study in any mode other than by distance (Candela et al., 2009; Fuller et al., 2014). The study sites or knowledge projects of some researchers (e.g. anthropologists, archaeologists, ecologists, marine scientists) may force them to be based far away from campus when conducting their fieldwork. Some doctoral researchers may spend a portion of their enrolment away visiting another institution or laboratory. Others may be committed to living and working in one geographic location but their preferred supervisor/s and/or institution are elsewhere.

STUDENT VOICE: "I would never have been able to afford to study full time on campus nor had enough support to help with my caring responsibilities. Distance study gave me an opportunity to reach the highest level of education that most people of my age, gender and socioeconomic background are usually barred from."

Many students take up distance study in order to accommodate busy and demanding lives, including professional and/or caring responsibilities (Butcher & Sieminski, 2009). While we explore this juggling of multiple responsibilities in Chapter 4, it's worth noting here the importance of distance doctoral pathways for students whose doctoral ambitions need to be slotted in around existing commitments that have to happen in a particular place (Burford & Hook, 2019). Distance study can act as a key pathway for women in particular, who in some social contexts are at risk of exclusion from doctoral education due to the uneven distribution of care labour (Bireda, 2015). Distance doctoral modes are therefore important from an equity perspective, making doctoral education accessible to people who may otherwise miss out.

Some students' choice of distance or flexible study modes may relate to their own health status (physical or mental) or disability. Perhaps accessing a university campus is inconvenient, impossible, causes anxiety, or feels unsafe. For such students, studying from home can make managing both health and a doctorate doable.

> **STUDENT VOICE:** "With a chronic illness, [as a distance student] I was able to rest at home in between bursts of activity. I don't think I could have done it if the expectation was that I would be 'at work' every day."

Other students' main reason for wanting to study at a distance is simply that they prefer it. Perhaps they like the autonomy, find the buzz of campus too distracting, or just fully embrace the joys of working from the comfort of home. Distance study can be something we genuinely want and choose, not just something we have to settle for!

In our 2022 survey, the key reasons why students said they undertook a doctorate by distance were simple. The majority didn't live near their institution, and studying by distance was best for them. COVID-19 was another common reason, highlighting that not all students who are engaged in distance doctoral research will necessarily have *chosen* this as their preferred pathway. Around a quarter of our survey respondents said that distance was the only way they could make study possible, and many noted that they valued the reduced environmental impacts associated with not travelling to and from campus each day. All these diverse reasons show why it's so important that distance study modes be both available and well supported for doctoral researchers.

> **STUDENT VOICE:** "For me, [distance] is the only way to balance my responsibilities as a parent and researcher. I don't have access to a quiet space that isn't shared, which affects my productivity. But I like having all my resources at hand and not having to commute. Also, it helps me to be available if there are any problems or emergencies at my children's schools."

Finding a university and a supervisor with distance in mind

This section is written for those who are still making choices about where to study. If you have already begun your distance doctoral journey, you might skip ahead to the next section.

For those anticipating distance doctoral study, a first key step is to do some homework and acquaint yourself with some of the general expectations of doctoral level research. There are several good advice texts (see the "Useful resources" list at the back of this book) that can help you understand what a doctorate is all about, how it's different from undergraduate and Master's work, what it might take to complete a doctorate, and the challenges and feelings you might expect along the way. If possible, also speak to one or more people who have actually *done* a doctorate, or are working on one; in the age of social media, you might know someone who knows someone in this category who might be willing to talk with you over a coffee. Alternatively, as a prospective doctoral student you can join some of the online groups (see "Useful resources") for doctoral students and others in academia, and learn from others in those communities. Taking these steps to learn about the nuts and bolts of the doctoral experience can help make the doctorate seem more real. This is important for all students, but perhaps especially so for first-generation students.

Next, identify the possible institutions you want to apply to. Often, multiple ingredients go into making this decision. You might consider the reputation of the institution and the specific department; the match of the department with your interests; and available supervisors and how their expertise relates to your research interests. Depending on your circumstances, you may also need to consider the country the institution is in (including any visa or relocation considerations) and the available research funding, stipends, and/or scholarship opportunities. Perhaps there are specific opportunities you want to take up during your doctoral degree, such as teaching experience, an industry internship or mentor, or an international exchange or mobility programme that you also want to consider, depending on your priorities and aspirations. Or perhaps you have a particular disability, learning need, or other form of diversity, and you need to find an institution and/or supervisor that will be equipped and willing to support you effectively.

From a distance perspective, it's important to investigate regulations and practices at your selected institution/s around distance, hybrid, and online modes of doctoral study. Use the university website, talk to the graduate office, and ask questions of your prospective supervisor(s). How will supervision happen? Will you be required to attend campus for certain milestones (e.g. induction, confirmation/upgrade or oral defence)? Also probe the support available for off-campus students (e.g. library support, researcher development, student learning services, postgraduate association, access to research culture opportunities like reading circles or workshops) and in any other areas relevant for you (e.g. off-campus provision for additional language learners, part-time students, disabled students, mature students, student carers, or neurodivergent students). Some institutions may have strengths or reputations in particular areas, although it is always worth talking to some current or recent students about their experiences rather than relying on how this institutional support is portrayed on marketing materials.

How you actually seek doctoral admission differs across contexts. For example, some institutions have set application windows, whereas others consider applications on a rolling basis throughout the year. Some but not all institutions require you to secure a supervisor before applying. This means it is important to read the institution's website and associated guidance carefully so that you approach admission appropriately. And always, *always* follow the application instructions! Often, applications are screened out because they don't contain the required information or didn't follow the specifications that were set out.

In some contexts (and particularly in social science and humanities disciplines), the initiation of doctoral projects tends to be guided by the individual interests of doctoral students. In these cases, doctoral applicants typically develop a research idea and then approach prospective supervisors seeking a mutual match in interests. Faculty and departmental websites will contain listings of academics and their contact details, often with a searchable index of keywords or areas of expertise. It's worth investigating the research interests of the supervisors you are approaching—look at their publications, their online profiles, the work of Master's and doctoral students under their supervision, and the areas in which they teach. Many universities also have online research repositories where you can learn more about individual researchers, read some of their publications, and access theses completed under their supervision.

You would then email potential supervisors to inquire if they are interested and available. While this is just an email, these small texts can have an inflated significance. Supervisors might read a lot into these messages, forming an impression of who you are, your research interests (and whether these link to theirs), your professionalism, and even your potential as a scholar (Kier-Byfield, 2022). We recommend that you make sure the email comes well in advance of an application deadline; write in a way that is courteous and informative, introducing you and your proposed topic; and tailor it to the individual receiving it (e.g. demonstrate that you have engaged with the prospective supervisor's research and that your work aligns with theirs).

> **STUDENT VOICE:** "Ensure you spend time selecting your supervisors, as much as they select you! This was advice shared with me and it really made all the difference. Having supervisors who could work via distance and provide that level of support makes the process much easier."

On the other hand, in some contexts (and particularly in science disciplines), the initiation of doctoral projects tends to be guided by supervisors who might advertise positions with specific topics or teams. If you are applying to join an existing research project or group, ensure that you find out as much as possible about the project or group, its focus, and the collaborators before applying. Make sure you are eligible to apply by looking at the selection criteria or person specification—don't waste your own or a supervisor's time applying for a place you could never be offered. Some doctoral opportunities may be open to international, national, or only local applicants, or only to those with qualifications in a particular discipline or topic area. Part-time study and/or distance ways of working may or may not be allowable, and partial residency might be required even for distance modes. There may be non-negotiable academic or language requirements. There may even be demographic requirements, such as age, ethnicity, or gender; while in some settings it may be illegal to recruit or screen on such grounds, in other contexts research funders may have specific requirements that a project needs to adhere to (e.g. inclusion of Indigenous research team members).

When communicating with prospective supervisors, it's important to remember that in some contexts doctoral admissions can be rather competitive and your email could be just one of dozens of possible applicants that the supervisor has received. This is why first impressions are crucial! Students will also often attach materials like a curriculum vitae (CV) and a draft research proposal outlining your research topic, research questions and proposed methods (for further practical guidance see Denscombe, 2012). Prospective supervisors will understand that your idea may still need refinement, but sharing such materials will give them an idea of your interests, academic writing ability, and potential to conduct independent research. Looking good on these fronts will help your email stand out from others this supervisor might receive.

Getting off to a flying start

So, now you're enrolled, have supervisor(s) and a (possibly still tentative) research topic. The "clock has started" on the multi-year project of gaining a doctoral degree. At this point, it's not unusual to feel a mix of excitement, overwhelm, and disorientation. After all, there are loads of new things to learn, people to meet, systems to figure out, and ways of working to establish. The sheer size of the doctoral project can also feel daunting, or the submission date may feel so far away that it's hard to see how your actions at this stage might help get you to that point.

The initial transition into doctoral study can be stressful and full of challenges for students generally as they position themselves in a new context (Golde, 1998). This often involves learning how and when to seek help, understanding the degree of "ownership" and autonomy a doctoral student has in their project, and diplomatically navigating new and sometimes complex power hierarchies (Grover, 2007). While campus-based students may have opportunities to quietly observe conversations that help reveal or explain some of these contextual factors, distance students may need to be more intentional in seeking out information that helps them adjust. You can aid your transition by being proactive, asking questions, and cultivating peer networks early (see Chapter 7). In addition to developing peer connections, previous research has found that developing high quality supervisory relationships (see Chapter 6), being aware of sources of advice and support, understanding relevant information about a new institution, and accessing training and development programmes can all assist new doctoral researchers to adapt well (Jackman et al., 2022). The activity at the end of this chapter is designed to help you gather this key information.

Of course, you'll also need to start the work itself—the actual intellectual project that will form the heart (often the whole) of your doctoral degree. How you start this work might vary from project to project, but it might include getting stuck into reading relevant literature, learning about new programmes or equipment, taking courses on ethics, and revisiting your research proposal/plan and any research questions that you may have embarked with. You might like to work through a tool such as

Tara Brabazon's *PhD Setup Document.*[2] While you may not feel ready to answer some of the questions such a resource poses, "doing things before you're ready" is to some extent inevitable in doctoral study, as we discuss in Chapter 5! The goal in using a tool like this is not to get it "right" but to stimulate the kind of purposeful thinking and conversations with your supervisor that will launch your project with momentum and energy.

Starting your doctoral work well will also require that you organise your life to accommodate the demands of your research and ensure you are able to progress at the necessary pace. The next two chapters can also help you think about how to get started in this regard.

As well as settling into a doctorate in general, though, you're also settling into a particular institutional and departmental context. To help you do this effectively, it's important to find out if orientation or induction sessions are available—and to sign up! Many institutions have begun offering online options and/or recordings for these sessions. If yours doesn't, you could try to get to campus or reach out and ask for an accessible pathway. It might be tempting to consider skipping orientation sessions. Maybe you feel you are too busy, or perhaps being fresh from previous study you wonder what extra there could be to learn. However, we'd caution against any sense that there is nothing left to learn as you transition into doctoral study. Formal institutional orientation sessions and more local level inductions can offer important opportunities to get off on the right foot. They are chances to connect with other researchers (who may be future collaborators or online coffee buddies), gain information that will help you throughout your degree, and learn how to access the support you might need through your studies. If there isn't a formal orientation or induction session available, perhaps you can ask your supervisor(s) or another member of your department if someone is available to give you an informal introduction to the key things you need to know.

STUDENT VOICE: "Get a support network in place as early as possible. Get familiar with all the resources that your university can provide (and don't be afraid to make use of them or let pride get in the way): click through every single section of the university's website; look at email bulletins to find out who's who and what resources are available. Find out who the administrators of your school/department/college are—they can answer many questions and often know who to ask if they don't. If you have a student union or student representatives for your course/school/department, get to know who they are and don't be scared to ask them questions either (they can also give more useful advice if things aren't right than staff can). No one will ever grudge answering a 'quick question'."

One of the things that can be difficult as a distance student is to learn to "read the university"—after all, to distance students, *the university* may feel far away or may simply look like a lot of websites and links to video calls. However, getting to know your institution is a key step in getting started. For example, at the beginning, there are often loads of acronyms to learn. Some of these differ from country to country, such as whether you are referred to as an HDR (higher degree by research student; Australia) or a PGR (postgraduate researcher; UK). Other acronyms and terminology vary from institution to institution. While this might seem like unnecessary jargon, getting yourself acquainted with your institution's specific language can help boost your sense of identity, belonging, and confidence within your new environment. Don't be afraid to ask for clarification or explanation of terms and acronyms.

It is well worth trying to develop your own "map" of your specific university. Each university is different, and there will be different pockets of support and community in different areas. It's your task as the doctoral student to use your excellent research skills to help you sniff them out! Your institution's website will probably be a key source, so plan to spend some significant time browsing and searching this site. In addition, induction workshops (discussed above), your department's postgraduate administrator or student services team, and/or your school of graduate research are also rich sources of this information. Your supervisors *may* also be helpful here, but we would suggest not relying solely on them: institutional policies and support offerings do change over time, and it can be hard for supervisors to keep on top of everything that is available or every current policy and procedure. While your supervisor may be able to point you in useful directions, we suggest you take responsibility for doing your own research on your institution's offerings and ways of operating. It's a good idea to take the view that "you don't know what you don't know", and also to remember that institutions change over time. As such, it's best to keep asking questions, reading newsletters, attending workshops, talking with other students, and checking websites and guidelines periodically even as you move through your doctoral years. You might just discover some new form of support that you didn't know was out there, or some new policy or procedure that you didn't know was going to be relevant to you.

As you research your institution, it may help to think of yourself and your project as being in the centre of an onion. The people closest to you in your doctoral journey are in the circle surrounding you: your *supervisor(s)* and (depending on national context) perhaps a *committee* that supports you through an upgrade process or your final examination. The next layer out is your *school, department, faculty or research centre*. Here, you'll have a number of colleagues (both fellow doctoral students and other academics), and there may also be a director, administrator, or coordinator responsible for graduate research in this setting—if so, these are key people to be aware of!

The final layer of the onion is the *institutional level*. This is where lots of central university support is based, which (having likely paid the same fees as everyone else!) you should have equitable access to as a distance student. Let's start with *librarians*, who are often the unsung heroes of research. Getting help to access materials is a key role librarians play. Most universities now subscribe to online research resources (e.g. journal databases, collections of online books) that distance doctoral students can access from anywhere (as long as you have access to adequate internet bandwidth). However, there are always things you can't access this way, and in Chapter 1, Jamie and Katrina both described having librarians send them books or scan relevant chapters. But access to resources is not the only thing librarians do. Librarians may also manage "open" repositories of resources where you might place your work and access the work of others; they may give advice on where and how to publish; advise on data management; and offer training on topics like literature reviews and searches, research metrics, and so on. As such, librarians become key resource persons in your research and, while they are not meant to do your research thinking and searching for you, they are there to support you when you get stuck.

> **STUDENT VOICE:** "What helped me was a very supportive and speedy library service by my uni — chat functions, librarians easily available via email, straightforward procedures on how to request for resources, having the option of requesting postage of paper copy resources to my residence."

Staying at the institutional level, *research offices* or *researcher developers* may offer additional support through research-focused workshops, seminars, and initiatives. These units might focus on areas like productivity, research practice and methodologies, writing and language support, guidance on managing supervision relationships, and career development. Some universities have *analytical facilities* that employ consultant statisticians. *Language or student learning centres* at universities often support doctoral researchers in developing their academic writing skills. *Accessibility services* or *disability support services* are important to make contact with early; often these services are open to supporting students in a wide range of circumstances. Many universities also offer *mental health and wellbeing support* (for more on caring for your health and wellbeing, see Chapter 5). Finally, your institution may have *support networks or mentors* for particular groups of students (e.g. faith-based student groups; Indigenous student mentoring; postgraduate student associations; international student networks and more).

As a distance doctoral researcher, it is important to learn what your institution offers and how it structures support services. Only then you will be able to know *who* to ask for *what*. While many of these research support facilities were only accessible to on-campus researchers in the past, more and more of them now offer their services online to accommodate a greater array of researchers' needs.

> **STUDENT VOICE:** "[Strategies I used included] linking with a broader network of people, especially for activities that promoted focused work or learning (e.g. shut up and write sessions, writing retreats/groups). These opportunities were offered or promoted through the university, and helped by creating a routine where I knew that certain times of the week guaranteed focused work."

Activity: Induction checklist

This checklist is designed to help you get off to a flying start with your doctoral programme. It's organised into two parts: connection building and information gathering. However, it's likely that these parts will merge. For example, as you make connections with others, you'll probably discover useful information; as you explore your institution's website, you may discover additional ways to build connections with key support people. If you can't find information signalled here, turn to your connections and ask for guidance.

Connection-building checklist

- Connect with your supervisor(s) professionally and early. Invest time building a relationship and discussing how your supervision might work, including distance elements, since effective supervision relationships begin with clear expectations (for more, see Chapter 6).
- Email the director of doctoral studies in your department/ area introducing yourself and your project. Let them

know that you are not on campus but are keen to be a part of what is going on in your department community.

- Connect with the doctoral or postgraduate student administrator. Find out about their role and ask how you can best stay informed about departmental news and activities.
- Reach out to other support services (e.g. library, student learning) and groups (e.g. mentoring, international network) to learn how they can support you as a distance doctoral student. Ask about what is on offer and how you can stay up to date with information and activities from these groups.
- Begin building connections with fellow doctoral researchers. You may meet some through student groups or orientation events; alternatively, your supervisor(s) may be able to connect you with one or more of their other students. See Chapter 7 for more ideas around building your networks.

Information-gathering checklist

Policies and administration:

- Where can you find policies and guidelines surrounding doing doctoral research at your institution?
- What is the process for making changes to your candidature (e.g. suspensions or changing the rate at which you study)?
- Who do you contact if you need to extend or vary your scholarships or funding?
- Are there policies or frameworks for progress monitoring (e.g. confirmation/upgrade and/or annual reviews)? When do these happen, and what do you need to do?

Learning and progressing:

- Are there policies or guidelines for how postgraduate supervision should work? How does the university define the student and supervisors' roles?
- What processes must be followed in relation to research conduct (e.g. ethics, integrity, data sovereignty, biosafety)? How do you access the training that is most relevant for you?
- What university units (e.g. library, student learning, graduate/research school, subject departments, and IT) contribute to professional learning and training for doctoral researchers? What do they offer? How do you access these supports at a distance?

The thesis:

- How many words/pages do you need to write for your thesis?
- What thesis formats are possible at your institution or in your department? Which format/s are likely to suit your project, and what do you need to know about them?
- Can publications be included in your thesis? If so, what regulations govern this?
- Where can you find information on how your thesis should be formatted?

Submission and examination:

- What is the required timeframe for submitting your thesis? What variation is possible?
- What are the regulations related to professional editing and proofreading of theses?
- How does thesis examination work at your institution? What criteria will be used?

Resources and support:

- What programs or sessions are available to support your development as a researcher, and how do you stay in the loop about these opportunities? Are there off-campus options for them?
- What resources are available to you as a doctoral candidate? These could include: stipend, funds for research expenses, travel/conference funding, IT equipment, software downloads/licences. How do you access these? Which resources require approval, and who from? (E.g. your supervisor(s) or a depart-mental administrator may have to approve spending of research funds, while access to certain software may be an automatic entitlement).
- What health (including mental health) and wellbeing supports are available, and how can you access them? If you need to register to be eligible to access health and wellbeing services, consider doing this now! If you find yourself in some sort of crisis later in your enrolment, the paperwork involved in registering with student health in order to access support may feel overwhelming. However, if you complete the enrolment now, then you are ready to go if it is ever needed.
- Where can you seek support with a dispute, a supervi-sion breakdown, or a situation requiring legal advice?
- What career guidance, support, and training services are available?

Notes

1   We recognise that the words *thesis* and *dissertation* are used differ-ently in different contexts, and that there are also different forms of

doctoral output (e.g. creative practice plus exegesis). In this text, we mostly use the word *thesis*, reflecting our own backgrounds, but you should consider our advice as applying to whatever your doctoral project or text will be called.

2   www.academia.edu/81853216/Taras_PhD_Set_Up_Document

References

Bireda, A. D. (2015). Challenges to the doctoral journey: A case of female doctoral students from Ethiopia. *Open Praxis*, *7*(4), 287–297. https://doi.org/10.5944/openpraxis.7.4.243

Burford, J., & Hook, G. (2019). Curating care-full spaces: Doctoral students negotiating study from home. *Higher Education Research & Development*, *38*(7), 1343–1355. https://doi.org/10.1080/07294360.2019.1657805

Butcher, J., & Sieminski, S. (2009). Enhancing professional self-esteem: Learners' journeys on a distance-learning Doctorate in Education (EdD). *Enhancing the Learner Experience in Higher Education*, *1*(1), 44–45. https://doi.org/10.14234/elehe.v1i1.7

Candela, L., Carver, L., Diaz, A., Edmunds, J., Talusan, R., & Tarrant, T. A. (2009). An online doctoral education course using problem-based learning. *Journal of Nursing Education*, *48*(2), 116–119. https://doi.org/10.3928/01484834-20090201-02

Denscombe, M. (2012). *Research proposals: A practical guide*. Open University Press.

Fuller, J., Lowder, L. & Bachenheimer, B. (2014). Graduates' reflections on an online doctorate in educational technology. *TechTrends*, *58*(4), 73–80

Golde, C. M. (1998). Beginning graduate school: Explaining first-year doctoral attrition. *New Directions for Higher Education*, *101*, 55–64. https://doi.org/10.1002/he.10105

Grover, V. (2007). Successfully navigating the stages of doctoral study. *International Journal of Doctoral Studies*, *2*, 9–21.

Jackman, P. C., Sanderson, R., Haughey, T. J., Brett, C. E., White, N., Zile, A., Tyrrell, K., & Byrom, N. C. (2022). The impact of the first COVID-19 lockdown in the UK for doctoral and early career researchers. *Higher Education*, *84*(4), 705–722. https://doi.org/10.1007/s10734-021-00795-4

Kier-Byfield, S. (2022, July 13). Pre-application doctoral communications and gatekeeping in the academic profession. *HE Education Research Census.* https://edu-research.uk/2022/07/13/pre-application-doctoral-communications-and-gatekeeping-in-the-academic-profession/

3 Outer work

Organising life, time, and space for distance doctoral research

So, you're a doctoral student working at a distance. You might have been working this way for some time, or you may be just settling into this mode of study. Maybe you have bought yourself some new stationery, a sleek Bluetooth keyboard, some appropriately scholarly slippers, or a jaunty writing hat! But, despite your official "student" identity, perhaps little in the environment that surrounds you has changed so far.

In this chapter and the next two, we address the challenges and opportunities of becoming a doctoral student when you are away from campus life. This chapter considers the practicalities of life, time, and space and how these might be particular for distance students: (i) framing up the doctoral project as knowledge work and explaining why it can be hard to keep everything balanced, (ii) setting time aside for your studies (iii) planning tools and strategies, and (iv) creating space for yourself as a doctoral scholar. Chapter 4 considers how we juggle doctoral work alongside intersecting employment, family, care, or other responsibilities, and Chapter 5 delves into the "inner work" that accompanies the practical aspects of a doctorate, exploring how this can take place when we're off campus.

DOI: 10.4324/9781003334088-3

Doctoral research is complex knowledge work

Completing a doctorate is a once-in-a-lifetime, multi-year effort to break through the edges of existing knowledge. You will discover previously unknown insights and communicate these ideas, along with the integrity of your research process, in a substantial scholarly format that will be subjected to robust scrutiny by respected scholars. Only around 1% of the world's population holds a doctoral degree (World Bank, n.d.), so it's no small thing!

Research is a form of *knowledge work*. Clark and Sousa (2018, pp. 12–13) highlight some of the characteristics of knowledge work that are helpful for us to understand:

> Inputs bring no guarantees of outputs in knowledge work, [and] success is determined only by what is produced: years can be spent working to no discernable success, while a mere moment of insight can be groundbreaking … The success of knowledge work depends on *getting the right things done*, then acquiring the knowledge to do the next right thing (Drucker, 1967). Due to the demands of others, time is always insufficient for knowledge workers to do all that could be done. Success involves making the right choice of what to do.

Do any of these points sound familiar? Working on a doctorate is messy, and we constantly have to make decisions about what to spend our time on. We can easily lose swathes of time on not-very-important tasks (perhaps related to filing, highlighting, or editing) that make us feel like we are working but do not actually bring us closer to completing our research. There are also a range of knowledge work activities that we must choose how, whether, or when to engage with. Writing academic articles or book chapters, presenting at (or organising!) conferences, serving on committees, undertaking sessional academic work, engaging in academic social media networks— none of these activities is inherently unwise, and each of them can add to our scholarly development, potentially enhancing the quality and/or completion pace of our doctoral work. You'll see we even recommend each of these activities as beneficial elsewhere in this book! However, these activities can also become distractions or forms of "productive procrastination" if they stop us progressing our doctoral project. This is part of the greedy reality of knowledge work, and we are best equipped to navigate this reality if we are aware of it.

Getting real about time and planning

The diverse personal, educational, and professional backgrounds we bring with us enrich our doctoral projects. Some of us might enter doctoral study with well-honed time management and planning strategies developed in previous careers, as parents, or through volunteering in community organisations. If so, we can and should bring those familiar strategies forward to help us manage our doctoral work. Others, however, might bring less confidence in managing our time and planning our way through big projects. The ways we have typically worked in the past might not have actually *worked*, so we might want to consider ditching some of them and learning new ways of operating as we embark on our doctorate.

Time is a notoriously sneaky substance. It can seem to slip by too quickly; other times, it's as if it's dragging on. Different cultures make sense of time differently. For some, time spent on doctoral work might be a precious retreat from other cares, or a welcome focus after having rather too much unoccupied time. For others, doctoral time is snatched and hard-fought amid the chaos of jobs, children, household tasks, community responsibilities, and more.

Some of us may feel that knowledge creation cannot be rushed, and our financial and other circumstances may allow us to let the doctorate stretch out in front of us. We may wish to resist the neoliberal emphasis on rapid doctoral completion and refuse to be "told" (by supervisors, the institution, or books like this one) how fast we should progress. In the later stages of enrolment, the doctorate may become a place to hide, as we postpone the challenges of seeking employment or conceptualising a new research project by simply delaying our doctoral completion. Others, in contrast, are highly motivated to complete the doctorate in the most efficient way possible—perhaps in order to make best use of a scholarship, obtain the coveted "Dr" label that will unlock our next career step, or get this darn thesis out of our lives! Still others sit at neither of these extremes but may aspire to a way of working that helps get the doctorate done (and done well) without serious damage to our health, wellbeing, career, or important relationships.

We believe it is important to open up time management and planning for conversation. How we manage ourselves in relation to time is so often hidden away from public view, and we don't think it should be! While academics are often good at waxing on about our substantive topics of interest, we often pay less attention to the micro-practices of how the work gets done and how we encourage ourselves into doing it.

Being based off-campus brings both advantages and disadvantages in terms of figuring out how to "work like a doctoral student". Off-campus, we often have fewer opportunities to observe other doctoral researchers in order to develop a sense of how much time to commit, and when to do what. We may not have such ready access to officemates who can offer positive examples, benign accountability, or lessons learned from being a few steps further along the journey. However, on the plus side, when based off-campus, we are not restricted by campus facilities' opening and closing times, car pools and commutes, or the rush for available parks. We are also shielded from getting swept up in the social momentum of lengthy ritualised coffee breaks on campus, extended conversations centred on complaints and task-avoidance, or confusing "time spent in the office/lab" with "actual progress made on my thesis".

> **STUDENT VOICE:** "In many ways, being a distance student is helping to prepare me for the life of a creative writer. It has taught me how to independently research and write, yet also be part of a writing and scholarly community. I have had to learn to manage my time, resources and working conditions. It has given me the flexibility to do all this while also being a functioning family member, businessperson and surviving a worldwide pandemic."

There is no doubt that effectively managing time is key to successful and timely doctoral completion. Some students will be on scholarships that end after three or four years, yet a large proportion of students are not ready to submit by the time their funding runs out. Perhaps this is why time management is so frequently included in research on the key areas of professional development that should be offered to doctoral students (Bromley & Warnock, 2021). Poor time management is often identified as a source of anxiety and distress for doctoral students (Virtanen et al., 2017). Doctoral students call on multiple sources of support to assist them in learning about time management, including supervisors, external coaches (Godskesen & Kobayashi, 2016), and mentors (Fulton et al., 2018). However, around half of doctoral students still report not knowing how to manage the time and tasks involved in a doctorate (Katz, 2016). Sussing out our relationship with time can be a tricky thing for doctoral students to learn, and yet it is a core part of managing ourselves during a period of largely independent study.

How much time do you actually have?

We encourage you to get curious about time and your relationship to it: to understand when you get wishy-washy or flaky around time, to identify some of the (perhaps unconscious) factors and pressures that shape how you work with time, and to locate some habits you wish to embrace. A good first step is to check the institutional expectations around time within your specific doctoral programme. (Ideally, you would know this before signing on to the degree, but this may not always be the case!) Timeframes to look out for include the amount of time (roughly) you may be expected to commit to your studies per week; the dates/times of any compulsory course-work or seminar events you plan to attend; any doctoral milestones you may need to meet (e.g. an upgrade or con-firmation of candidature, a pre-submission review); and your expected and maximum dates of submission. You might learn about these expectations during your orientation or through a conversation with your supervisor(s); the expectations might also be written in your offer of study letter, or stated in a policy statement. Once you have a sense of the number of hours you have agreed to commit to your programme of study, you are in a better position to organise your life, be intentional about how to make the best use of those hours so that your research progresses well, and give yourself a break if you find you are already working at or well above these expectations.

The next thing to consider is *when* you will be studying and how you will establish a routine. Some people treat doctoral study as akin to working at a job. They prefer a disciplined approach, working regular daytime/weekday hours, and ensuring that they take time off in the evenings and weekends to recharge and recuperate. For distance students, the "doctorate-as-job" approach has benefits: it means there is regular time set aside for doctoral study and the boundaries between study and work can become clearer. Given that doctoral time is notoriously "leaky" and can take over our whole lives if we aren't careful, it can be useful to define exactly which times are *not* going to be filled with doctoral work. Our friends and family are likely to appreciate us having (and honouring) these boundaries.

On the other hand, many distance students squeeze doctoral study in around work, family/care commitments, and/or a disability or illness, and so taking the "full-time job" approach may not be possible or desirable (see Chapter 4 for more on this "juggling work", and see Rainford & Guccione, 2024, for more on managing part-time doctoral study). Ultimately, there's no single "right" way to complete a doctorate or organise your weeks. The key thing is to figure out what is right for you (and for right now—it may change over the course of your doctorate) and try your best to put that routine into action. Planning a routine might not mean that things unfold as planned every day or every week, but it does mean that, on balance, you have organised your life in a way that means that there is a doctorate-sized space available where you can do research.

STUDENT VOICE: "Motivation is particularly tricky, I find; having a routine helps, though. I also would say that [if you] think about the average workday, you aren't working the whole 8 hours, there's coffee, and breaks, and chats with neighbours etc. Don't feel bad if you are doing laundry or other things around the house in "work time" … Time to think is important, and research and writing is done even when you aren't sitting at a computer etc. So long as you are meeting your goals and deadlines then you are doing good."

No matter your situation, it is important to be honest (with yourself) about the times you will be studying and the times you will be doing all the other things a complex life involves. Be realistic and think about your actual lived life—not a fantasy life that you hope you might have!

STUDENT VOICE: "Be kind to yourself on some of those days where you just want to curl up and do nothing. Work smart, not hard. Your willpower and creativity are limited resources; be sure not to force them to the brink. Small goals and light bites get the meal done."

If you are working from home, doing a doctorate can easily be mistaken for having plenty of interruptible time. Your family, friends, or work colleagues may be anywhere along the continuum of supportive to hostile regarding your decision to undertake a doctorate. They may also have only a vague idea what doctoral research involves. Since family and friends are important support systems for doctoral researchers, it might be worth having a conversation to help your loved ones understand what you are embarking on. You could outline the kinds of changes they might expect for you and your availability in the coming years, and ask for their help in supporting you as you commit to your doctorate (see Layton, 2016, for a good example of this). There's more on how you might have these conversations in Chapter 4.

Time zone differences are a final time-related consideration for some distance students. It can be difficult to participate in a workshop at a time inside "working hours" for those on campus but when you have already changed into your pyjamas. As one student put it in our research study, "online events just didn't happen when my brain was able to engage". If you find yourself in this situation, you might approach your supervisor(s) or the organisers to see if more time-zone-friendly timings could be considered.

Activity: Calendar audit

Part 1: Your actual week

Sit down with a week-per-view calendar and look at the shape of *your* typical week. Fill in all the things that are currently a part of your life: mealtimes, childcare, commute, meeting friends and family, school committees, community and voluntary responsibilities, paid work, health and wellbeing appointments, sleep, exercise, housework, rest/free time, and so on. What does your week look like? Is it crammed full, or an open expanse of white space? Once you have the existing contours of your life plotted into your calendar, you will have a better sense of the time you might have to get your research work done.

Part 2: Your ideal week

Now try to map out an ideal week that lets you fit in your doctoral work while balancing this with other things you value. What would it take to hit the approximate number of hours that your institution recommends for your mode of study? What options do you have for how this might look? What might suit you (and your family) best? And what might actually be realistic? There's nothing worse than mapping out a plan that's so tight it requires you to be superhuman. As soon as "life happens" or you have a low-energy day, the plan goes out the window and you're back to your old ways. Try to create a plan for an ideal week that you think you could actually maintain.

If this exercise reveals that you have less time available than you expected or need, then you have some choices to make. Are there areas where you could reduce your commitments to create time for the doctorate? Could you renegotiate childcare arrangements, pay for a cleaner or gardener, or step down from some voluntary or leadership roles? Some of us might encounter greater constraints or diminished wellbeing if we were to say "yes" to any of these questions, so consider not only what will be possible for you but also how each possible approach is likely to affect you.

It's a good idea to revisit this exercise periodically, e.g. when your regular doctoral progress review milestones roll around or as part of a personal New Year's audit. Circumstances change over the course of a doctorate, and so your plan will need adjusting accordingly. Our own time practices can also "drift" easily, making a deliberate review helpful for keeping us on track. Be kind to yourself, though, if circumstances outside your control get in the way of your doctorate for a period. This is unfortunate but all too common (see Chapter 8). At times when you're simply unable to devote a full-time amount of attention to your doctoral research, varying your study load (e.g. changing your enrolment to part-time) can be strategic so that your candidature time won't slip away underutilised.

Productivity and planning

In addition to managing our *time*, another aspect of planning is managing the *tasks* that make up the doctoral project. For some of us, planning can feel like treacherous territory surrounded by stormy seas of guilt, shame, and disappointment. Some of us disregard planning or think it is not for us. Maybe we think of it as trying (and failing) to fit into rigid boxes that can never contain the mysteries and magic of true human experience. But what if planning wasn't simply discipline and punishment? What if you conceived of plans as support structures that you are in control of and that exist to assist you to think and work well? What if not every plan was supposed to be completed exactly like it says on the page each and every time?

> **STUDENT VOICE:** "I think being organised and maintaining good structures around my work has made study via distance a lot more achievable. I definitely struggle sometimes but if I know what I'm supposed to be doing then it helps. This I have just learnt through time and working out how I work and trying different strategies."

Plans can keep you "anchored" and help break up the mammoth task of completing a doctorate. They also help protect you from some of the traps associated with know-ledge work that we discussed earlier (such as putting in lots of hours at your computer but not coming away with any meaningful forward progress). Plans can remove some of the "decision fatigue", if you've mapped out (for example) at the beginning of a week what you need to accomplish each day. Combining planning with digital tools that automate reminders can be helpful for any doctoral student, but perhaps especially for those with conditions such as ADHD who need concrete scaffolds to help them manage and direct their own efforts.

When you're working from a distance, having a clear plan that is mutually negotiated and regularly reviewed is especially important to help make sure that you and your supervisor(s) have a good idea of the course that your doctoral journey is taking. Many of Katrina's research students (both distance and on-campus) keep a copy of their timeline/s at the front of a shared supervision records document, to ensure everyone keeps sight of this important plan.

We have learned three big lessons about planning. First, *different kinds of plans are needed, at different scales, for different things*. Longer-range plans are for bigger goals, like when you want to finish writing a thesis draft. Medium-range plans are, not surprisingly, for medium-sized things, like when you aim to finish a thesis chapter or paper. Smaller plans then help you work toward these larger goals and decide what to focus on in a given week, day, or block of study time. Planning across these multiple levels and making sure that each plan feeds into the others can be extremely helpful.

The second big lesson about planning is that *things can change, and plans can, too*. Given the amount of time doctoral research takes, there are often unexpected changes either within or outside the research project itself (see Chapter 8 for more on dealing with this). Some will be outside our control; for example, the COVID-19 pandemic demanded significant change and flexibility in the plans of many doctoral researchers. Our plans therefore need to be living/working documents that we return to and adjust in response to both progress and circumstances.

The third big lesson concerns *prioritising*. A common tendency among doctoral students (and most humans!) is to prioritise *less* important things before *more* important things. It can be extremely tempting to spend a lot of time checking emails, formatting documents, or downloading articles, but this can distract us from ever getting to the important tasks. Instead, we encourage you to try scheduling time for the most important things initially, then letting smaller bits and pieces follow afterwards. The activity at the end of Chapter 4 can help you think more about this, as can Kearns and Gardiner (2013).

STUDENT VOICE: "I used a lot of pomodoros and other structured time techniques as well. Lots of goal setting (and making those goals public through Twitter) to keep me accountable and moving forward on the project."

Jamie and Tseen have worked with students who were focused on accelerating toward completing their doctorates. The ideas below are based on some of the planning and management strategies that students identified as particularly valuable.

- Is it helpful to shift your focus from inputs (endless time at your desk/computer) to outputs (tangible progress towards completion: words written, sections edited, data collected or analysed, articles read and summarised)? Like much knowledge work, doctoral tasks can expand to fill up whatever time is available. It is helpful to use clear tasks and microgoals to ensure that the time you invest moves you forward in meaningful, measurable ways.
- Could "habit stacking" (Clear, 2018) help you shift into doctoral mode more easily? For example, you might always write in the same physical space; equip yourself with the same things (a cup of coffee, a consistent writing playlist, or even—to take a leaf out of Jamie's book—a "writing hat"!); and/or engage in a consistent initial practice such as taking three deep breaths, writing down your intention for the day, visualising yourself productive and in flow, or saying a prayer or blessing over your work session. Stacking several such habits together strengthens the effect of the signals sent to your body and brain.
- Might you help smooth your way into work sessions by leaving hooks or "notes to self" when you end a session? Try writing down a really specific "next thing to do" to allow you to dive back in when starting a new work session. This can help avoid losing a chunk of time re-reading everything you'd previously written and wondering what to do next.

- If "to-do lists" and "weekly plans" keep going wrong or make you feel guilty or stressed out, could you try recording what you *do* accomplish each day/week/month (sometimes called a "to-*done* list")? This way, you can track your measurable outcomes and celebrate all you're achieving. You can also look back to get a sense of how you've been spending your time, allowing you to identify gaps or obvious improvements.
- Can you create extra time? Normally, time is the one thing we cannot generate more of but, in your doctoral programme, you may have the option to suspend your candidature or to switch between full-time and part-time study. These changes push out your submission due date, creating extra time. Students sometimes worry that taking these steps might reflect negatively on them but, in reality, these are very common adjustments that many students make as life unfolds during their doctoral enrolment (see Chapter 8).
- Do you wish to explore the "slow" (Berg & Seeber, 2016) movement in academia?[1] It resists the academic culture of busyness, pressure, and speed in favour of deep thought, wisdom, and balance. It's important to be wise and not use this movement as an excuse to put your head in the sand and avoid the challenges of doctoral work, especially since institutions have increasingly rigid doctoral completion timeframes, but we suggest it's possible to find a middle path that balances being productive with being calm.

Ultimately, our advice would be to get curious about your own practices with personal management and productivity to better understand how you work. This is not only something that is valuable for the doctorate; it's valuable knowledge to have across a whole career.

Creating space for yourself as a distance doctoral student

Doctoral research is an embodied and spatial practice, and the environments around us matter. As past studies have outlined (Dowling & Mantai, 2017; Promsaka Na Sakonnakron & Burford, 2020), ordinary knowledge work like reading, writing, doing experiments, and collecting data is inescapably spatialised and emplaced. While doctoral students who work primarily on campus may be assigned offices, labs, or other spaces to work in, becoming a distance student often involves making choices about the locations where you'll undertake doctoral work.

STUDENT VOICE: "I love my office! It has become a more sacred space through the PhD journey. It has held me. It is private. I could not imagine doing the writing part of the thesis in the shared, impersonal and transitory offices that might have been available to me. I could not imagine making the library my writing home either—uncomfortable, insecure, too many visual distractions, always feeling seen and in public. Research and writing are for me very personal."

Your home may be a key workspace for you. Many doctoral students turn areas of their homes into fruitful sites for their doctoral studies, but it is important to acknowledge that distance doctoral students will be making choices within varying horizons of possibility. Some of us might live in houses with good internet connections and spare rooms, sleepouts, or other spaces that could be used for doctoral work. That's great! Others of us may live in busier homes, or homes which have more constrained possibilities for physical workspace. There's potential here, too. We might make use of a kitchen table, a hallway, or a small partitioned area at the top of the stairs that's in reach of the WiFi. The key thing is to think creatively about how you can make the best possible (comfortable, productive, and ergonomically safe) study environment in your setting. If you know you need quiet to focus, how will you minimise distractions in your environment?

> **STUDENT VOICE:** "Make sure you have a comfortable (good chair, standing desk ideally), inspiring working space, outside of your bedroom [if possible]! I do find it necessary to separate work from home physically to avoid overworking or procrastinating."

Many doctoral students draw on their own ingenuity to make home spaces work for them. For example, one Australian doctoral student and sole parent transformed her walk-in wardrobe into a home office to complete her doctoral work during the school day (Burford & Hook, 2019). She worked in her closet because it was small and economical to heat, and because it enabled her to close the door on her doctoral work and move into parenting mode when her young son was home.

Doctoral students also work in public spaces such as cafés, libraries, trains, airports, and the lobbies of art galleries and hotels. We can look for spaces that suit us best: those who flourish when surrounded by people and white noise might choose to work in a coffee shop, while those who need peace and quiet might go to a local library or co-working space. Working outside of the home can be energising if we're stuck in unhelpful patterns (e.g. "housework procrastination") or always working in the same place is feeling stale. And sometimes, our spatial choices link to our time landscape—as a full-time working mum and part-time doctoral student fighting for time to work on her research, Katrina regularly had her laptop on her knee at the hairdresser!

STUDENT VOICE: "The silence afforded by my bedroom was more beneficial than the shared office I have at work."

There's no doubt that finding ways to organise your life, time, spaces, and research tasks is a central part of navigating your distance doctoral journey. In this chapter, we have tried to outline different approaches to time management, productivity, planning, and workspaces. We know every student's circumstances are different, so we've highlighted different contexts and offered various possibilities for how you'd get things done. We hope you'll try some things and see how they work for you; you can always go back to your previous methods (or try something else new) if you find something doesn't work for you!

A final caveat: While it's good to be focused, well-organised, and ambitious, it's also important to recognise that you are not superhuman. You do not have a magic wand, time turner, or Tardis, and your doctorate will not write itself with no time investment. Not even you can fit 48 hours of work into a 24-hour day, and you certainly can't survive for three years with no sleep. None of us can devote the *whole* of ourselves to our paid work, family, or care responsibilities AND work full-time on a thesis.

For most doctoral students, it's a constant negotiation as you look to be the best possible steward of your time and energy. The ideas in this chapter and elsewhere in this book can help you do that, but if what you're aiming for is simply beyond the bounds of possibility and reason, a bigger rethink is required. In that scenario, we recommend seeking advice from a counsellor, graduate school advisor, wise mentor, or trusted family members as you look honestly at what you're trying to accomplish and make some tough decisions about what you can genuinely do within the 24-hour days, 7-day weeks, and 52-week years that we all have to work with.

Resetting your ways of working

There may come a time when you realise that you are stuck. Perhaps you've fallen into unproductive patterns of working, and those patterns have been reinforced and reinforced through repetition—many years of repetition, even! Or perhaps time management strategies, planning approaches, or workspaces that have been effective for you in the past no longer seem to be doing the job. If this is you, take heart. It's not over, but it is likely time for a reset.

As we highlighted in Chapter 1, there are lots of areas in which you have agency around how you undertake your doctoral work. This means that if ways of working are no longer actually *working* for you, YOU are (in most cases) the one with the power to change them! It's important to give yourself permission to make the changes needed in order for you to succeed. Shifting tack is not an admission of failure, but rather a natural part of taking responsibility for your life and your doctoral work. The doctorate is a journey that changes us (more on this in Chapter 5), and so it's not unreasonable that it might change the ways we think and operate.

In some cases, just recognising that your current practices aren't serving you well can be enough to shake you out of your inertia and prompt you to try something different. The ideas in this book can be a resource to return to any time you recognise that this sort of adjustment is needed. Completing some of the activities we've provided can help you step beyond just perusing our ideas and start actually making sense of how they can apply in your particular situation.

If you need more support and input to achieve a productive reset, that's fine, too. Remember that you are being brave in showing up for yourself in this way, admitting that you need assistance, and being willing to try new things in order to persevere with the ambitious and important doctoral project that you have chosen to undertake. Your university may offer access to counselling, coaching, or advising (outside of the supervision relationship); if so, these spaces can be invaluable for thinking through the reasons you are stuck and what might help you progress. Student learning tutors or researcher development staff at universities also often fulfil this role, so check their website or contact their administrator to ask what help they can offer you. Your university might also offer workshops aimed at doctoral students on topics such as project management, planning, or academic writing (these often deal with the behavioural and psychological aspects of actually getting ourselves to write, not just the grammar and style aspects). These can be helpful both for the content you'll learn and for the chance to be among a group of students all facing some of the same challenges.

Other sources of support when a reset is in order include family, friends, and anyone in your wider circle of acquaintances who you would consider as a mentor. They don't need to know much about doctoral research to be able to help you think through your situation—especially if you arm them with a copy of this book! If funds allow, you could also make use of independent professionals such as counsellors or coaches, although do be wary of the academic coaching industry that has popped up in recent years. Never engage (or pay for the services of) an academic coach without an initial consultation to see what they offer and if you feel a sense of relational "fit", and ideally also seek references from real students they have supported.

Finally, as this book illustrates, there is an extensive "advice literature" out there for doctoral students, which can help you reset. Some of our favourite resources for students in need of mindset and/or behavioural shifts include YouTube videos from Tara Brabazon's series of 300 "vlogs" for doctoral students; Brabazon's (2022) book *Comma: How to Restart, Reclaim and Reboot your PhD*; Katherine Firth's (2020) book *Your PhD Survival Guide: Planning Writing, and Succeeding in your Final Year*; and the resources by Hugh Kearns and Maria Gardiner at https://www.ithinkwell.com.au/.

Activity: Exploring your strategies for success

The questions below are designed to help you reflect on your relationships with time, space, motivation, and your research work. They could be used in peer support sessions; in conversations with key support people; or individually by writing down or speaking aloud your responses.

Time, planning, and organisation

- Do you have "golden hours" or "sparkly brain" time when you find your focus and/or creativity? Are you an "owl" who works best later in the day or at night, or a "lark" who works better in the morning/earlier in the day? If possible, try to use your best time for the best kind of activity.

- If you tend to plan in quite large chunks (e.g. complete thesis chapters, your whole research project, or a full year of study), try identifying smaller goals that add up to the larger goals. How does mapping these smaller elements influence your motivation to complete a task?
- Are there new tools you want to learn about? Do you prefer paper planners, notebooks, whiteboards, or digital platforms for managing your tasks and commitments? How can you set up a planning and/ or task tracking system that you'll enjoy using and be more likely to maintain?
- Are there specific times, or uses of time, that really help you feel connected to other researchers, your supervisor(s), your institution, or wider research communities? How and why might you prioritise these?
- If you are disabled, neurodiverse, or facing other challenges (e.g. mental health difficulties), have you talked with your university's accessibility services team? They may be able to suggest tools that could help you manage your workload, priorities, time, and attention effectively.

Motivation and accountability

- Rewards can be a really important part of motivation. How do you build in rewards and reinforcements to celebrate when you have done a job well?
- Does keeping a record of what you have done (e.g. time spent, papers read, page/word counts) work for

you? Many students keep not only a "to-do" list but also a "done" list so that they have a motivating record of their progress.
- What sources of accountability do you have in your life? Where can you find positive accountability that doesn't induce guilt or panic but helps you remain focused on "keeping first things first"?

Space and boundaries

- Where do you work best? Do you work better in particular places for particular types of task? What could you change about your workspace(s) to better support your wellbeing and productivity?
- Is your research work clearly separated from other areas of your life, or are the boundaries blurred? Is research "leaking" into family time, leisure/wellbeing time, or holidays? Do you have a space where you can focus on your research without being distracted by others? Are you finding you are physically present at home but mentally still engaged in your research? How can you more clearly decide when and where your research work happens, and also how you step away from it?

Note

1 See also https://theslowacademic.com/, https://thesiswhisperer.com/2011/07/11/slow-academia/, and https://thesiswhisperer.com/2018/05/02/slow-academia-is-for-the-privileged-but-then-isnt-all-academia/

References

Berg, M., & Seeber, B. K. (2016). *The slow professor: Challenging the culture of speed in the academy*. University of Toronto Press.

Brabazon, T. (2022). *Comma: How to restart, reclaim and reboot your PhD*. Author's Republic.

Bromley, T., & Warnock, L. (2021). The practice of the development of researchers: The "state-of-the-art". *Studies in Graduate and Postdoctoral Education*, *12*(2), 283–299. https://doi.org/10.1108/SGPE-12-2019-0084

Burford, J., & Hook, G. (2019). Curating care-full spaces: Doctoral students negotiating study from home. *Higher Education Research & Development*, *38*(7), 1343–1355. https://doi.org/10.1080/07294360.2019.1657805

Clark, A., & Sousa, B. (2018). *How to be a happy academic*. Sage.

Clear, J. (2018). *Atomic habits: An easy and proven way to build good habits and break bad ones*. Avery.

Dowling, R., & Mantai, L. (2017). Placing researcher identifications: Labs, offices and homes in the PhD. *Area*, *49*(2), 200–207. https://doi.org/10.1111/area.12317

Firth, K. (2020). *Your PhD survival guide: Planning, writing, and succeeding in your final year*. Routledge.

Fulton, A. E., Walsh, C. A., Gulbrandsen, C., Tong, H., & Azulai, A. (2018). Doctoral student mentorship in social work education: A Canadian example. *Studies in Graduate and Postdoctoral Education*, *9*(2), 98–112. https://doi.org/10.1108/SGPE-D-17-00046

Godskesen, M., & Kobayashi, S. (2016). Coaching doctoral students—A means to enhance progress and support self-organisation in doctoral education. *Studies in Continuing Education*, *38*(2), 145–161. https://doi.org/10.1080/0158037X.2015.1055464

Katz, R. (2016). Challenges in doctoral research project management: A comparative study. *International Journal of Doctoral Studies*, *11*, 105–125. http://ijds.org/Volume11/IJDSv11p105-125Katz2054.pdf

Kearns, H., & Gardiner, M. (2013). *Time for research: Time management for academics, researchers and research students*. Thinkwell.

Layton, D. (2016). Being my own coach: Achieving balance in the four domains of life. In Frick, B. L., McMaster, C., Murphy, C., & Motshoane, P. (Eds.). *Postgraduate study in South Africa: Surviving and succeeding* (pp. 115–126). African SunMedia.

Promsaka Na Sakonnakron, S., & Burford, J. (2020). Doctoral students' readings of the politics of university office space. *New Zealand*

Journal of Education Studies, 55, 165–180. https://doi.org/10.1007/ s40841-019-00149-w

Rainford, J., & Guccione, K. (2024). *Thriving in part-time doctoral study: Integrating work, life, and research.* Routledge.

Virtanen, V., Taina, J., & Pyhältö. K. (2017). What disengages doctoral students in the biological and environmental sciences from their doctoral studies? *Studies in Continuing Education, 39*(1), 71–86, http:// doi.org/10.1080/0158037X.2016.1250737

World Bank. (n.d.). *Educational attainment, Doctoral or equivalent, population 25+, total (%) (cumulative).* https://data.worldbank.org/indica tor/SE.TER.CUAT.DO.ZS?view=map

4 Juggling work

Distance, research, employment, family, and care responsibilities

One of the things that's great about distance study is that being off-campus can enable us to pursue our academic goals while maintaining important family, care, social, employment, and cultural responsibilities. If you're in full-time paid or voluntary employment, distance study allows you to fit your research work into the spaces around other (typically less flexible) obligations. Pursuing your doctorate off-campus might enable you to be the parent you want to be, attending your children's school field trips or performances and being there for drop-offs and pick-ups. Working from home could be the only option when you are engaged in part- or full-time care for loved ones who are ill, injured, disabled, or have limited mobility. If you are actively involved in serving or supporting your local community, distance study can allow you to remain engaged in that community rather than relocating in order to base yourself nearer to your university campus. We've even heard from doctoral researchers who choose distance modes of study to ensure that their beloved pets are not left home alone day after day!

DOI: 10.4324/9781003334088-4

> **STUDENT VOICE:** "Distance gave me the opportunity to do a doctoral degree. It gave me flexibility to work when I could, whether that was 4am before the kids woke up, or during nap time. It gave me the opportunity to be at home with my children while they were young and spend a lot of time with them. Being on campus would have been easier and faster in some ways (I took 7 years to complete), but I would have lost that strong bonding time."

This chapter rests on the assumption that each of you will have made choices about what roles and responsibilities are important or necessary for you to maintain. Even if you did not "choose" (for example) to become pregnant, for someone you love to become ill, or for others to refuse to contribute to caring for a mutual loved one, there is agency in you choosing to step up and become the carer that you know someone needs to be. So, we will *not* be telling you that you "can't" have a baby during a doctorate (Katrina did), that you "can't" juggle a doctorate with caring for an unwell parent (Jamie did), or that you "can't" complete a doctorate while parenting and maintaining a full-time job (Katrina did!).

Instead, we want to help you think about the landscape of your unique circumstances and to feel a sense of agency in considering strategies for balancing your doctoral work, your other responsibilities, and your wellbeing. To do this, we cover: (i) the "greedy" nature of academic, employment, family, and community obligations; (ii) strategies for finding your own path; and (iii) the role of others in navigating boundaries and decision making.

Academia, employment, family, and community: "Greedy" institutions

Academia, employment, family, and communities all enrich our lives and help us be our full selves. However, they are also "greedy" institutions (Coser, 1974) placing enormous, poorly bounded, and ever-expanding demands on us. Even with conscious time management and decision making, each has the potential to consume our time, energy, and productivity. This can leave us feeling overwhelmed, and may ultimately threaten our doctoral completion, relationships, and/or health and wellbeing (Sverdlik et al., 2018).

If you're reading this chapter, then you are probably living in the intersection of a doctorate and some significant other responsibilities—or you're considering this in the future. Being in this intersection likely comes out of what you value. For example, you may value pursuing a doctorate (for intrinsic reasons like the joy of learning or personal satisfaction, and/or for extrinsic reasons like career advancement or peer esteem) but also value the opportunity to start a family, contribute to caring for others, be at home with your children, continue your career, be active in your faith community, or engage in other activities. The challenge is not to strip away any of these values but, rather, to find a balance that works for your circumstances, commitments, and values. Thinking this through is relevant for all doctoral researchers, but it is likely to be particularly important for *distance* doctoral researchers who may have less obvious boundaries between "home/domestic life" and "research" than those who work on campus regularly.

> **STUDENT VOICE:** "[A challenge from the multiple roles I juggle is] not having defined boundaries between my research work and my home life. This induces feelings of guilt if I am working but know that there are household chores or caregiving tasks to do. And guilt when I am doing the housework or caregiving because I'm not working on my doctorate. I can't say I have overcome these barriers. I think I've accepted that's just how it is for me, and I try to do my best not to fail at everything."

In Chapter 3, we described research as a form of knowledge work where there is always more to (potentially) do than we have time for. In this chapter, we consider how this "greedy" characterisation may also apply to our other responsibilities. We do not want to paint a depressing picture of overwhelming, inescapable obligations; rather, we hope that honestly considering the nature of your particular obligations, values, and priorities will help you gain perspective and move with agency towards developing a balance that is most right for you.

Employment responsibilities

For some of us, there is simply no choice: we have to work during our doctoral enrolment in order to pay the bills. Our job(s) must remain a top priority to protect our financial security, and our doctoral work gets some of what's left over. Others choose to continue working alongside doctoral study, perhaps because of the satisfaction we get from our employment; our values; the expectations of those around us; or a resistance to letting the doctorate be the only thing we have in our lives. For others still, the separation between employment and doctoral study may be blurred, such as when undertaking an industry-based or professional doctoral programme.

> **STUDENT VOICE:** "The main opportunity [associated with completing my doctorate via distance] has been the chance to continue to work in my field, and in one of my jobs I was able to combine my study with my work. This wouldn't have been possible if I was a full-time student attending campus. Distance does provide for more freedom as far as studying at your own pace and time."

Work environments and conditions vary greatly across countries, sectors, seniority, and specific employment contracts. You will be well aware of the "must-do" elements of your employment responsibilities and how these define the ways you spend your time. Your work may stay comfortably within the expected hours, but it is equally possible that it leaks into additional time and spaces. This might result from picking up extra shifts, taking work home to meet deadlines or catch up, unreasonable workloads or staff shortages, perfectionism, anxiety about meeting expectations, or even your own choice to offer extra time because it's work you care deeply about. Those on fixed-term contracts carry an additional mental load, continually looking ahead to what might happen when a contract ends and spending time pursuing subsequent employment opportunities.

At times, our work patterns change for a finite period, such as if we pick up overtime or extra duties. However, if you are in an ongoing pattern of what feels like unhealthy over-working, perhaps the first step is to pause and take an honest look at the situation. What is the root cause? Will the situation resolve itself, or is some assertiveness or action from you going to be required? What would you like to see happen? Some coaching, therapy, or training may help you think through alternative boundaries or strategies for managing your work. Conversations with your manager(s) could add perspective or allow for shared problem-solving. Changing jobs may make all the difference to your wellbeing as both an employee and a doctoral researcher. Revisit your priorities: What would you be willing to shift so that you protect the time and space for your doctoral research and other important commitments?

We know that this juggling act is far from simple, and that fear, anxiety, perfectionism, self-doubt, a desire to please others, and the complex power dynamics within workplaces can be deep-seated drivers of our behaviours (Van der Bijl, 2016). As academics ourselves, we each struggle with many of these same tensions around the "slice" of our lives that we allow our paid work to occupy. We each also have (or have had, at different times) our own family, care, community, and social responsibilities, which we turn to now.

Family and care responsibilities

Family and care responsibilities are undoubtedly "greedy", with poorly defined task boundaries compounded by the strong emotional bonds we have with those we care for. There is always more that can be done when managing a household or caring for others, and there is always more quality time that could be invested with those we love. Murphy (2013, p. 25) aptly speaks of the "kisses between paragraphs" that may make you feel torn and guilty but equally can help sustain you and your loved ones throughout your doctoral journey.

Carers, especially parents and primary carers, can find themselves "always on". Even when they expect to have some precious uninterrupted time for their doctoral work, there is always the chance of a phone call requiring a sick child to be collected from day care or school; a health emergency meaning the carer has to stop working and take their loved one to the doctor or hospital; a change in another carer's circumstances necessitating stepping in to cover their absence; or an urgent request for foster or respite care for a child in need.

There are well-documented inequities in the distribution of family and care responsibilities. Women often shoulder higher physical and mental loads associated with parenting, managing a household, and caring for others (Goldin, 2021; Power, 2020), and there is no doubt that this intersects with doctoral study (Lourens, 2016). Women's caring responsibilities also tend to be "sticky": it can be difficult for women to mentally disconnect from their care responsibilities even when they are physically elsewhere (Henderson, 2021). Those living in poverty, from marginalised groups, from lower socio-economic communities, or from Indigenous communities also often carry disproportionate care workloads (Oxfam, n.d.). Those in mid-life increasingly find themselves part of the so-called "sandwich generation", simultaneously engaged in caring for their children and their parents (Vlachantoni et al., 2020); single parents carry heavy loads without a partner's contribution. Different countries offer vastly different policy and welfare support for parents and carers, and those from disadvantaged groups are most affected by the deficits in such policies worldwide (International Labour Organisation, 2018). Finally, on a more practical level, those who do not have available support networks (such as co-parents, grandparents, or other family members) are likely to carry heavier care loads.

Many doctoral researchers work off-campus precisely *because of* their family and care responsibilities, with distance making it possible to engage in both research work and care work. There also seems to be a particular intersection between part-time and distance modes of study, since both modes cater well for students with family, care, and/or community responsibilities (see also Rainford & Guccione, 2024). If you're parenting or caring for others while undertaking your doctorate, you're certainly not alone. However, some of the challenges are likely to be *feeling like* (or being made to feel like) you're on your own; supervisors and/or institutions not understanding the reality of your circumstances; and managing the competing, "greedy", "sticky" demands of research and care work.

Community, social, and cultural responsibilities

Other commitments can also become demanding or even "greedy". You may choose (or be expected) to serve, lead, or even just attend a lot of events within your extended family, faith community, or cultural group. Volunteer work, cultural leadership, advocacy, or governance roles may occupy some of your time and headspace. Alongside your doctoral work, you may want or need to earn enough through your paid employment to not only provide for your own immediate needs or for your family but also be able to give money to others. Alternatively, financial or other forms of material support (including things like help with childcare) may be flowing *towards* you from your wider family or community right now, on the understanding that once you have completed your doctorate you will be actively "paying back" and "paying forward" the privilege of your higher education. There may also be strong expectations from others (e.g. community leaders) about what you will research and the contribution your study should make to your community or cultural group. Each of these things will impact in unique ways on your time, further reinforcing the importance of finding effective strategies to balance your multiple roles and responsibilities. The rest of this chapter focuses on how this might look.

Finding your own way

Part of completing a doctorate is discovering and developing your academic identity (explored further in Chapter 5). This process includes finding ways of managing your time, prioritising, making decisions, and resting that reflect not only your academic goals but also your underlying values and wider responsibilities. As Markides (2020) shares in her beautiful autoethnography, "Driving: The Unseen Responsibilities of a Doctoral Student, Mother, and More":

> My identity is in flux between my roles as teacher and student, wife and mother, writer and researcher, Métis and activist, chauffeur and more. I traverse the ground of responsibilities, deadlines, expectations, and commitments, daily. The competing demands take a toll on my physical body … I am more than the sum of

my academic accomplishments: more than my
trips to the university for teaching; more than
my research journeys and conference travels;
and more than my accumulated publications.
(pp. 133, 142)

Purposeful efforts to exert agency in relation to our time,
our priorities, and our multiple roles and responsibilities are associated with doctoral student wellbeing and
balance (Martinez et al., 2013). We suggest that finding
your path requires two types of work: *conceptual work*,
as you find ways of thinking about and making decisions
around your research and other commitments, as well
as *practical work*, as you find the strategies, practices,
and "life hacks" that allow you to stay on track. Either
conceptual or practical work on its own may help, but
we think both can help you achieve your goals and live
in accordance with your values. This chapter is deliberately sandwiched between Chapter 3, which tackles the
practical work of managing life, time, and space, and
Chapter 5, which delves into the deeper, more conceptual
work of considering your values, identities, and wellbeing.

Activity: Finding ways to juggle—and flourish!

Below are a range of practical ideas that may be specifically helpful for those who juggle distance doctoral
research, employment, family, care, community, and other
responsibilities. Take some time to review these strategies, as well as the practical strategies in Chapters 3
and 5. Think of them as a menu, rather than a recipe. As

with any menu, there will be things you already love or are immediately drawn to try, things you may be interested in sampling, and things that you don't think will suit you. That's fine—as long as you're not closed to any/all practical changes that might actually help you! As you look at this menu, what would you like to sample? You might also like to return to the ideas periodically. Different strategies will work for different people and research stages, so give yourself time and space to experiment, and let go of any strategies that don't seem to work for you. You might return to this list periodically and find that something different stands out as potentially useful.

- Experiment and learn what practices really accelerate your doctoral progress. Then deliberately embed these things to help "supercharge" your research and offset the times when you are busy with your employment, family, care, or other commitments. For example, you might benefit from some of the research culture activities we describe in Chapter 7; academic coaching or counselling; more frequent supervision meetings; or even a weekly "Friday Update" email to your supervisor that lists (and holds you accountable for) what you've achieved in a week.
- Try doing some things *less well* and see what happens—either research tasks or in other areas of your life. Remember to check in regularly on how these decisions are working out for you. For example, many working parents are advised to just ignore having a house full of unfolded laundry, unwashed dishes, and clutter everywhere. Is this freeing for you? Does it help you focus on what matters to you? Or does the visual "noise" of all this mess actually bother or distract you continually and stop you feeling calm? There's no one

right path, so give yourself permission to explore what works for you.

- Find ways, big or small, to make life good now. So often, we go through life waiting for the next season, when life will finally be "good": when the kids have left home; when we've completed our degree; or when we've got that next promotion or pay rise. But when we cross these thresholds, things often aren't as we expect, and we are soon waiting for the *next* season! Consider the idea that *life can and should be good now.*[1] Not perfect, of course, but good. This might mean making practical changes such as cutting out surplus activities or protecting set times for distraction-free family, leisure, or self-care time.

- Regularly practising rest, gratitude, and mindfulness can help disrupt negative thought patterns so that you experience your life in the most positive way possible.

- Find ways to mark the boundaries between doctoral work and other roles/responsibilities. Perhaps this could be closing the door on your at-home workspace; choosing a landmark you drive past on the way home where you intentionally "shift gear" into family mode; or sticking to agreed times after/during which you don't work on your research.

> **STUDENT VOICE:** "Try and have a separate workspace or at the very least a shut down ritual where you finish work at the end of the day."

- Match tasks to the available time and opportunities. If all you had to do was your doctorate, you could align your work patterns with your personality and preferences—but if you're fitting your doctoral work around other things, you may not have the luxury of working in these "ideal" patterns. In the long run, you'll benefit from overcoming your mental rules around when you "can't" do good work and learning to work effectively in a range of circumstances. We recommend differentiating *deep work* (analysis, draft writing, substantive revisions/reshaping of material) from *surface work* (transcribing or entering data, checking references, formatting, proofreading, filing, and email). Deep work requires solid blocks of focused concentration, but perhaps some surface work could be done in between interruptions, while caring for or being available to others, or when you are tired. Target your deep work tasks in times where you're "off duty" in terms of care responsibilities. This might mean doing deep work in the morning when your children are at school and saving easier tasks for when they're home after school, while you're sitting outside sports practice, or in the evening when you're tired.

- Discriminate between golden hours and fantasy hours (Kearns & Gardiner, 2012):

> Fantasy hours are when you tell yourself (and others) that you are working on your research when in fact you are thinking about it but doing something else e.g. surfing the net, photocopying articles, renaming your folders. Real hours or golden hours are quite different. These are when you are engaging with the real part of the research. It could be writing. It could be analysing results. It could be trying to grapple with a really difficult concept. The good news is that two golden hours equals about ten fantasy hours … but they must be golden hours. (p. 30)

- Keep a close watch on yourself. If you find that you're sitting at your desk or computer but not being productive, recognise that you've slipped into the "fantasy hours" zone. This can stem from procrastination and distraction, but it can also reflect genuine exhaustion and overload for us super-stretched "human givers" (Nagoski & Nagoski, 2019, p. 4). In these cases, rather than desperately continuing, listen to the signal that your body and mind need some rest and refuelling. You can return once you're ready to give "golden hours" again.

STUDENT VOICE: "With an already busy schedule, organisational strategies have been key. I maintain a physical 'to do' diary which lists all the tasks that I need to undertake, both for my job and for my PhD. I can then cross these off as they are completed. It enables me to see at a glance which days are heavily committed and when I can realistically fit in my PhD activities. The nature of my job means that there are peaks and troughs, dictated by various deadlines. These are identified first, along with supervision dates and assignments so that I can manage my time to ensure that everything can be completed to plan. Sometimes work has to take priority and at other times my PhD takes priority."

Navigating boundaries and shared decision making with others

As you seek ways to balance your doctoral work alongside your family, care, and other responsibilities, it's worth considering whether you can bring your partner or key support people (grandparents? parents? flatmates?) into your decision making. Undertaking a doctorate will require sacrifice and flexibility from anyone you live with; it will never be an "invisible" houseguest. If you are partnered, you probably involved your partner in the decision to enrol in doctoral study. Ideally, the shared decision-making should not end there. Proactive care and communication can help prevent resentment or an "expectations gap" that may otherwise fester over the years of a doctorate. It may be helpful to share this chapter with your key supporters. Together, you might engage in some of the conceptual work, do and discuss the activities, or browse the practical strategies and consider what might work for your unique situation. You will be the best judge of what is likely to be constructive, though—if you're well into your study already or have tricky relationships to navigate, you may already know that some people in your life resent your doctoral study and the attention it receives. You will have to judge whether it's likely to be possible to bring these people along, whether some professional input (e.g. counselling) might be needed to help resolve things, or whether it's better to minimise the emotional labour involved and just get your degree finished.

Children warrant a special mention. While completing a doctorate and thesis have sometimes been compared to growing and birthing a child, they aren't of equal importance! Your children (or those you care for) will benefit from being included in age-appropriate ways in reflecting on how things are going in the family; sharing the things that make them feel connected and loved; and understanding why you are spending all this time hidden away at your computer. The example you provide for your children through your hard work and learning can be inspiring, and children can become powerful allies and cheerleaders in your doctoral journey. However, if all they experience is a constant stream of "No, go away—I'm working" then there are risks of disconnection and sadness. What helps your children feel they have had quality connection with you? Parenting courses, family rituals, and dedicated time together can help you make sure you are living in line with your values.

> **STUDENT VOICE:** "Set time for your loved ones. I have a tendency to lose track of time when immersed in things I am interested in, but this is not so good for a marriage. Therefore, I learnt to make time for my husband over dinner, coffee, etc., and we negotiated the specific evenings that I could work. I also had to make time for my children and grandchildren, which was easier as a distance student in that I had more time flexibility but also harder as I was always home and, presumably, available, so I struggled a bit with the interruptions … I got a lot of work done in the evenings when there were less interruptions. I am SO glad that I did it!"

Finally, don't forget that your supervisors and institution are among the "others" who can help you navigate the challenges of your multiple roles. This is most likely to be important if things in the non-research areas of your life go seriously wrong (see also Chapter 8). A family member may become seriously ill; you might lose your job; or you could become involved in a highly stressful or challenging situation within your workplace, family, or wider community context. It can be tempting to just ignore your doctorate in these times, and we would certainly support you prioritising the things you value most (e.g. family, health/wellbeing) and taking the time you need to work through such situations. However, there are two key things to do in any crisis that arises during your doctorate. First, inform your supervisor(s). They don't need all the personal details, and you can choose a mode of communication that feels manageable and safe (e.g. a brief email may feel more comfortable if you're worried about breaking down while discussing the details on the phone or via Zoom). But your supervisors do need to be aware that you're dealing with something and need to pause your research work — otherwise, they may wrongly assume you're unmotivated, procrastinating, or not up to the demands of doctoral work. Second, make use of the pathways your institution has available for pausing (suspending) or stretching out (extensions; changing to part-time study load) your enrolment. In many institutions, you are not allowed to apply for these changes retrospectively once things are back on track. This means it's important to know (or ask your supervisors, administrator, or graduate research school) what options are available to you and then take action in a timely way if the worst happens. It may be the last thing you want to think about when your attention is being demanded in one of the other spheres of your life, but following these processes puts you in the strongest position to be able to resume your research down the track.

Staying positive amid the juggle

Doctoral researchers are to be found across all sectors of society: the carers and the cared-for; women, men, and non-binary people; the abled, disabled, and neurodiverse; all ethnic groups and nationalities; all socio-economic backgrounds; all countries of residence. More and more doctoral researchers hold family, care, and community responsibilities that enrich their lives and their research. As authors and researchers of doctoral education, just as we resist the assumption that distance doctoral study is somehow "second best", we also resist the idea that these broader responsibilities somehow detract from people's ability to do great doctoral research.

We've noticed that compared to their "unencumbered" counterparts, doctoral researchers who hold wider responsibilities are often more productive, better time managers, and more fulfilled, simply because they *have to* fit other things into their life and cannot allow their doctoral work to consume them. These busy, multiply committed doctoral researchers may bring sharp leadership, communication, or organisational skills that have been developed in their parenting, work, or community roles. Some may bring practical wisdom, deep insight, or particular empathy for others that can support their research work. Others may have a stronger sense of moral purpose driving them forward in their research. As supervisors, it is a privilege to walk alongside such candidates throughout their doctoral journeys and to see the whole-of-family celebration that comes with a doctoral graduation.

We encourage you to celebrate and take pride in the rich life you have woven together, bridging academic pursuits with family, care, community, or other responsibilities. There are synergies among these different domains and ways that these wider responsibilities shape you as a scholar. It is indeed possible to balance multiple roles well, drawing on the mix of conceptual and practical work described in this chapter as well as the practical strategies in Chapter 3 and the "inner work" we turn to in Chapter 5.

Activity: Rocks, pebbles, sand, and water

There's a well-known illustration that goes like this:

A speaker places a large glass jar on the table for their audience to see. The speaker asks a volunteer to come and fill the jar with rocks, asking the audience to decide when the jar is full. Eventually, no more rocks can fit into the jar, and so the audience agrees that the jar is now full.

The speaker calls for a second volunteer. This person is given some small pebbles and asked to add these into the jar. Despite the audience earlier determining that the jar was already full, the second volunteer is able to add a significant number of pebbles to the jar. The pebbles slip down through the cracks around the larger rocks and settle into the spaces between. The speaker asks the audience if the jar is now full; "Yes", they affirm.

A third volunteer is asked to add sand to the jar, which runs down amongst both the rocks and the pebbles. "Now," say the audience, "the jar really is full."

A fourth volunteer is given a jug of water. The volunteer pours water from the jug into the jar and, once again, the new material infiltrates the small spaces between the rocks, pebbles, and sand, and a jar that had previously been considered full is shown to be able to hold more.

Now the speaker asks the audience to think. "Imagine that we took everything out of the jar now, and separated the four materials—water, sand, pebbles, and rocks. We know that this quantity of material can fit into the jar, because we've just seen it. But let's say that this time, we put the water in first; then the sand; then the pebbles; and finally we try to get the big rocks in on top." The audience visualise this and realise that although the water, sand, and pebbles might fit, it would be impossible to get all the big rocks in on top or to push them down sufficiently through the other materials so that everything could fit.

The lesson is this: The jar represents our time, attention, and capacity. The rocks represent the things in our lives that matter most, such as our family and relationships, our health, and perhaps some of the most important tasks within our personal or professional lives. The pebbles are the next most important things, then the sand, and finally the water. If we make a practice of starting with our "rocks"—the things that we value most—we will find that we are able to honour and accomplish these things well and then fit in other tasks and responsibilities around the "rocks". But if we start with the trivial things—our "sand" and "water" tasks—we risk making it impossible to fit in the things we value most (our "rocks").

Draw yourself a jar filled with rocks, pebbles, sand, and water (or download a template from our website, www. doctoralresearchbydistance.wordpress.com). Label the rocks to name the things that are most important to you— the things that reflect your values and the kind of person you want to be. Then, below or beside the jar, list things that you would categorise as each of: pebbles, sand, and water. Keep your diagram somewhere so that it can remind you of the things you hold as most important, and work to put those "rocks" in *first* as you plan your week, allocate your time, and make decisions in the moment about your competing roles and responsibilities.

Note

1 Credit goes to Katrina's husband for this aspirational, challenging, but helpful perspective!

References

Coser, L. (1974). *Greedy institutions: Patterns of undivided commitment*. Free Press.

Goldin, C. (2021). *Career and family: Women's century-long journey toward equity.* Princeton University Press.

Henderson, E. (2021). Sticky care and conference travel: Unpacking care as an explanatory factor for gendered academic immobility. *Higher Education*, *82*, 715–730. https://doi.org/10.1007/s10734-020-00550-1

International Labour Organisation. (2018). *Care work and care jobs for the future of decent work*. www.ilo.org/wcmsp5/groups/public/---dgreports/---dcomm/---publ/documents/publication/wcms_633135.pdf

Kearns, H., & Gardiner, M. (2012). *The seven secrets of highly successful research students*. ThinkWell.

Lourens, G. (2016). Being a postgraduate woman: Relationships, responsibilities and resiliency. In Frick, B. L., McMaster, C., Murphy, C., & Motshoane, P. (Eds.). *Postgraduate study in South Africa: Surviving and succeeding* (pp. 101–113). African SunMedia.

Markides, J. (2020). Driving: The unseen responsibilities of a doctoral student, mother, and more. In Eaton, S. E. & Burns, A. (Eds.). *Women negotiating life in the academy: A Canadian perspective* (pp. 131–145). Springer.

Martinez, E., Ordu, C., Della Salla, M. R., & McFarlane, A. (2013). Striving to obtain a school-work-life balance: The full-time doctoral student. *International Journal of Doctoral Studies*, *8*, 39–59. https://doi.org/10.28945/1765

Murphy, C. (2013). Kisses between paragraphs: Strategies to maintain wellness during the PhD journey. *Early Education*, *53*, 24–26.

Nagoski, E., & Nagoski, A. (2019). *Burnout: Solve your stress cycle*. Ebury Publishing.

Oxfam. (n.d.). *Not all gaps are created equal: The true value of care work*. www.oxfam.org/en/not-all-gaps-are-created-equal-true-value-care-work

Power, K. (2020). The COVID-19 pandemic has increased the care burden of women and families. *Sustainability: Science, Practice and Policy*, *16*(1), 67–73. https://doi.org/10.1080/15487733.2020.1776561

Rainford, J., & Guccione, K. (2024). *Thriving in part-time doctoral study: Integrating work, life, and research*. Routledge.

Sverdlik, A., Hall, N. C., McAlpine, L., & Hubbard, K. (2018). The PhD experience: A review of the factors influencing doctoral students' completion, achievement, and wellbeing. *International Journal of Doctoral Studies*, *13*, 361–388. https://doi.org/10.28945/4113

Van der Bijl, A. (2016). Caught between work and study: Exploring boundary zones as an employed postgraduate student. In Frick, B. L., McMaster, C., Murphy, C., & Motshoane, P. (Eds.). *Postgraduate study in South Africa: Surviving and succeeding* (pp. 77–88). African SunMedia.

Vlachantoni, A., Evandrou, M., Falkingham, J., & Gomez-Leon, M. (2020). Caught in the middle in mid-life: Provision of care across multiple generations. *Ageing and Society*, *40*(7), 1490–1510. https://doi.org/10.1017/S0144686X19000047

5   Inner work

Identity, perspective, and wellbeing for distance doctoral researchers

So far, this book has considered what we might classify as "external" aspects of your doctoral journey: your enrolment, institutional context, management of time/space/tasks, and some of the other responsibilities you hold alongside your research. We now turn inward, considering how the doctoral journey makes us feel, affects our mental health and wellbeing, and transforms our identities. We also consider how students based off-campus might experience the pressures and enablers that can influence our inner worlds. Such "inner work" is important because being self-aware on our doctoral journey can enrich our experiences; accelerate our progress; equip us to navigate challenges and the unexpected; and hopefully make us better colleagues, friends, and family members thanks to our insight and self-regulation. Specifically, this chapter explores (i) the identity work involved in "becoming doctoral"; (ii) imposter syndrome and perfectionism; and (iii) nurturing your health and wellbeing.

The complexities of doctoral identity

Becoming a "Dr" is not just something that happens at the end of your studies when you stride across the graduation

DOI: 10.4324/9781003334088-5

stage. Rather, it is a process of identity construction that happens *inside you* across your doctoral studies:

> Identity is a notion that makes immediate sense to doctoral researchers. They feel themselves to be *in the process of becoming different*. Not only are they learning to be more competent researchers, but they will also be seen differently by others when they have the title "Dr" in front of their names. (Kamler & Thomson, 2014, p. 16, our emphasis)

The doctoral student is at once an insider-outsider-student-candidate-scholar-novice-expert who is expected to *learn* but also to *lead* an independent project. You have reached the pinnacle of the education system and your doctoral student status may be trumpeted proudly by your family and friends, yet in other contexts you may sometimes feel (or be made to feel) like an apprentice "at the bottom of the hierarchical academic structure" (Carvalho & Freeman, 2022, p. 7). Doctoral students are often not treated as true academics (McAlpine et al., 2014), and if you are working in a lab or research group, you may be acutely aware of the power distance between yourself and the senior professor leading the research programme. However, doctoral researchers should (by definition) be doing work at the leading edge of knowledge and innovation. You are an emerging "expert" and a research professional expected to work in a creative and independent way.

Doctoral researchers also often hold significant life experience and professional expertise, contradicting the idea that they are simple novices. In our survey of over 500 distance doctoral students, respondents' ages on beginning their doctoral research ranged from 21 to 71, with an average starting age of 37½! And alongside these complex and shifting identities, of course, sit the many other intersecting aspects of your identity. Perhaps it feels important to weave your scholarly identity in with other aspects, such as your faith, your sexual or gender identity, being disabled or neurodivergent, or a position such as being an antiracist, ally, or Indigenous scholar. Many researchers feel most fulfilled when their scholarly work intersects with other aspects of who they are. Nonetheless, it's a lot to grapple with on top of the academic challenges of a doctorate!

Your identity will shift as your research progresses: "As anyone who has undertaken a doctoral-level degree will tell you, doing a doctorate changes you" (Barnacle & Mewburn, 2010, p. 433). Writing autoethnographic poetry about her own doctoral identity journey, Leach (2021, p. 3) identifies multiple, incomplete identities-in-progress:

> My scholarly identity is being born in a series of in-between spaces. I am both in the academy and of it. I am in my graduate program's community and outside of it … The "I" in this narrative is fractured, not fully in one space and not fully whole.

This can be a challenging and perhaps unexpected element of the doctoral journey. You may find yourself caught between some of the competing positionings outlined above; you may notice such views subtly (or not so subtly!) underpinning the messages you receive from your supervisor(s), graduate school, or others in your department.

STUDENT VOICE: "Having had a baby during my PhD, and then experiencing mental health issues, I've come to appreciate my PhD in more ways than I anticipated. Studying is the thing that makes me feel like me. It is my consolation and my happy place. It is a huge part of my identity when the world wanted to brand me as 'mother'."

The changes a doctorate brings to how we think and communicate can also affect our broader life experiences, as Kamler and Thomson (2014) point out:

> Doctoral researchers often experience tensions in their personal relationships, tensions caused by the changes produced in and by the doctorate ... As [doctoral researchers] become more absorbed in an intellectual way of life, their ways of thinking about and being in the world change. (p. 16)

Thus, as we become increasingly doctoral, our political opinions may shift, or things that used to interest us may hold less appeal. Perhaps we become more difficult dinner party guests due to our questioning, complexity-oriented stance, or we find ourselves critically unpacking novels or TV shows in ways we just didn't before. We might also become more curious, determined, critical, organised, creative, and persuasive, all of which are key attributes associated with "doctorateness" (Bitzer & van den Bergh, 2014).

Get curious about how you feel—and how you are made to feel—within academia. Others may have reasons for trying to position you in certain ways in comparison to their own standing, and the ways you frame your own identity can support or inhibit your progress and wellbeing. Ultimately, you have some control over what you choose to absorb of the messages you receive from those around you. The next section considers how you might do just that.

Finding yourself: Becoming a doctoral researcher

Ongoing identity development is a normal part of life. What a doctorate offers is a powerful opportunity to turbocharge this work as we engage in deep reflection and growth across these intensive few years immersed in a big project.

As a distance doctoral student, you will likely have more space and separation from the identity constructions and expectations of others due to not spending as much time in the company of other researchers on campus. This space can bring greater freedom to consider who you want to become while simultaneously giving you less insight into the identity journeys of your peers. Realising that all doctoral students undertake this identity development can help you give yourself permission to do so, too!

Becoming a doctoral researcher is going to involve some identity shifts that you can anticipate, so embrace them! Initially, you might be leaving or reducing your previous employment to take up a doctoral place, shifting from an identity such as "manager", "leader", or "employee" back to what might feel like a "student" or "novice" role. You've chosen this, and even earning a doctoral place is a great achievement, so try to frame this first identity shift positively rather than apologetically.

As the doctorate progresses and you acquire new research skills and content expertise, new identities will be constructed. Perhaps you are becoming a *feminist scholar*, a *quantum physicist*, or a *critical realist*. It can be helpful to connect with other scholars who embody the particular identities you hold, such as other disabled or neurodivergent scholars, other first-generation doctoral students, or other Indigenous scholars; you may find these folks at conferences, in online communities, or through events (in-person or online) at your own institution.

Across the doctorate, you should also experience a broader move from your *student* identity to that of a *scholar, scientist,* or *independent researcher* (Bitzer & van den Bergh, 2014). Eventually, you'll overtake your supervisor as the ultimate expert on your specific topic!

An interesting development in research on identity over recent decades has been the idea that identity is *performed*. That is, we momentarily or more consistently "put on" different identities because we perceive that those are the identities needed from us in particular settings. For example, perhaps you've given a talk at a confirmation/milestone event or a conference, and you recall feeling nervous in advance but once "on stage" summoning what seemed like the right kind of scholarly voice and professional confidence to perform a *researcher-ly* identity for your audience. When communicating with your supervisor(s) or others such as academic librarians, you may deliberately seek to convey confidence and a sense that you are on top of your research field or thesis work. At other times, though, you may express a more hesitant, *outsider-ly* or novice identity, wanting others to recognise that you haven't done or learned something yet, or haven't been given the opportunity to do so. Perhaps you also describe your doctoral research differently to different audiences: you might tend to downplay your topic and/ or your expertise when talking with some friends, family members, or colleagues, yet present a more confident or excited picture when speaking with others.

The above are just some simple examples of how we all perform different identities across contexts and interactions. They demonstrate that our scholarly identity doesn't necessarily have to be something we feel "all the way down", all the time: there is a nugget of truth in the saying "fake it until you make it"! Doctoral researchers often need to transition into their new "expert" identity before they feel ready to do so (Kamler & Thomson, 2014). We suggest that rather than this being a poorly ordered developmental sequence (with tasks coming before you're up to them), it is in fact the case that *you develop your doctoral identity by doing doctoral things*. If you wait, you may never feel ready to start writing your thesis — but if you make a start, you'll develop your thesis-writing skills and confidence. The same is true for presenting at conferences, writing your first journal article, and going off to read about a thorny aspect of your methodology (rather than hoping your supervisor(s) will just "tell you the answer").

STUDENT VOICE: "Despite initial challenges working from home and feelings of inadequacy, I successfully defended my research proposal with the avid support of my supervisors and reviewers. This positive feedback has since given me confidence."

Writing is a key practice for doctoral identity work. When we write, we can "test out" a particular scholarly voice or identity, trying it on like a new item of clothing, considering how well it fits, and adjusting the fit or style as we edit and redraft. The process of writing "creates the scholar who at the end of writing is different from the writer who began. Perhaps a bit more knowing and confident, perhaps still worried about having something worthy to say, perhaps a bit bolder or willing to take greater risks" (Kamler & Thomson, 2014, p. 16). By sharing our writing—first with our supervisor(s), and later with examiners and the wider research community—we put our "scholarly identity out in the public arena" (p. 162). Writing in the form of journaling can also offer us a safe, private space within which to process the identity work we're engaged in.

Other things that research has shown can help build students' doctoral identities include producing research outputs (papers/book chapters), doing research work (e.g. experiments, reading, transcribing), talking about research (e.g. in seminars and conferences), developing academic networks; making intellectual and institutional contributions; and taking up responsibilities (Mantai, 2017; McAlpine, 2012). Engagement in sessional tutoring or marking work alongside the doctorate can also contribute to developing a rounded "academic" identity (for those who want this), since most academic careers span both teaching and research.

One of the biggest risks for off-campus doctoral students, in our view, is not realising the importance of activities such as those described above that may seem peripheral to the thesis but that are enormously powerful in shaping a scholar who can then create a strong thesis. However, knowledge is power. For example, if you are aware that giving presentations about your research can help you on your doctoral journey by building your doctoral identity, you can be proactive in looking for relevant conferences or seminar series (in person or online), planning for presentations, and considering things like funding or childcare so that you can attend. Try asking your supervisor(s) for leads around useful forums to present, network, or learn; asking your institution for a wider range of time options and delivery modes (including remote access and/or recordings) for events; and asking other doctoral students how and where they have tapped into some of these valuable experiences. If your institution hasn't offered these avenues to off-campus students in the past, remember that it sometimes only takes one doctoral student to speak up and ask for something to be different, more accessible, or offered in more than one way, for it to happen. You are also not restricted to your enrolling institution in terms of opportunities to network, present, co-author, or contribute to the academic community. Professional associations, online communities, cross-disciplinary, or cross-institutional communities and even your existing personal connections can be harnessed in ways that support your doctoral identity development (see Chapter 7).

STUDENT VOICE: "[Participating in workshops, academic conferences, and involvement with online support networks] made me feel part of a community, helped me to include 'researcher' as part of my own identity, [and] brought me motivation."

Overall, while doctoral identity development is a complex and fluid process, the crucial insight from identity theory is that it is through doing "doctoral things" that you will become increasingly doctoral. Don't wait to "feel doctoral" before attempting these transformative activities. And whatever you do, don't let "not feeling doctoral enough" become a form of self-sabotage, as we discuss in the next section.

Dealing with imposter feelings and perfectionism

Many doctoral students have track records as "high achievers". As a result, they may place very high expectations on themselves to do things extremely well. Pursuing excellence can be a wonderful attribute, and some people do have remarkable capacity to achieve great things. However, there are two key ways that these tendencies can become problematic among doctoral students: imposter feelings and perfectionism.

Imposter feelings involve self-doubt, a sense of unworthiness, and feeling like you're constantly at risk of being "found out" as a fraud because you and/or your work are simply not good enough (Addison et al., 2022). The hierarchical, competitive nature of academic environments can fuel imposter feelings for doctoral students, as can the challenges of conducting doctoral research itself. Chakraverty (2020) found that doctoral students' imposter feelings were particularly triggered by: progress reviews and milestones (e.g. confirmation/proposal defence), receiving public recognition, comparisons with peers, attending conferences, developing new skills or applying new knowledge, public speaking, academic writing, and asking for help.

Imposter feelings might cause you to question your abilities and achievements, misrepresenting yourself despite having clear evidence of your own capability (Kearns, 2015). Furthermore, as Ayres (2022) notes, "the particularly tricky thing about managing feeling like an impostor is that you likely think that everyone else is struggling from the Impostor Phenomenon, but you are the *real* fraud" (p. 86)! If not well-managed, imposter feelings can derail your academic progress and your wider wellbeing, including through self-sabotaging strategies like procrastination, perfectionism, overcommitting, and avoidance (Kearns, 2015). By living under the shadow of imposter feelings you might also rob yourself of the satisfaction of recognising and celebrating your own successes.

> **STUDENT VOICE:** "Don't take yourself too seriously—go into [your research] knowing you don't know everything but also believing you do know some things and your contribution is valuable. Imposter syndrome can be a struggle! But admitting what you don't know while holding confidently what you do know facilitates a more authentic learning experience."

At any career stage, humility and a learning disposition are always appropriate. However, the enormous number of senior academics who still report struggling with imposter feelings shows us that dealing with this particular issue is not simply about getting more experience. Ironically, Katrina and Jamie, who first drafted this chapter, both struggled with imposter syndrome in the process of writing about imposter syndrome and other aspects of "inner work"!

Being a woman, an older and/or international and/or first-generation student, having a disability, having a working-class background, or otherwise coming from a marginalised group are associated with feeling like an imposter in higher education (Addison et al., 2022). Imposter feelings can also intersect with perfectionism, which is itself another common challenge among doctoral students and academics (Ayres, 2022).

Perfectionism can develop out of imposter syndrome, as we tell ourselves that we just need to work harder, do better, and get things right in order not to feel like a fraud.

Alternatively, perfectionism might come first (or come with us into the doctorate) and cause us to overemphasise our failings and feel like we're never measuring up, which then fuels imposter syndrome. Unchecked, perfectionism can stop us even beginning a task because we don't feel ready to do it well enough—or stop us progressing to the next important task because we're never happy with the standard of the task we've been working on previously. Such self-sabotaging behaviours are common among doctoral students (Kearns & Gardiner, 2009).

Perfectionism may manifest in various domains of our lives. We might most commonly associate it with academic work, but perfectionism can creep into the pressure we place on ourselves to parent in a particular way, to manage our diet/body/finances/exercise/time/social obligations to particular standards, or to prevent our being enrolled in a doctorate from making any impact on the people we love or live with. Any of these forms of perfectionism can threaten our wellbeing and progress.

> **STUDENT VOICE:** "I am a perfectionist (not a funny ha-ha perfectionist, but a might-ruin-my-life perfectionist) and so I count getting the PhD to be one of the biggest successes of my life. It was extremely painful at times. Being a distance student did afford me a great deal of independence and autonomy, but this left me more alone with my demons. So I feel even prouder of having finished."

Overcoming imposter syndrome and/or perfectionism is likely to be an ongoing process, and you may need a combination of everyday, practical strategies as well as ways to shift your underlying thinking (Kearns & Gardiner, 2009). For example, you might:

- Develop a critical mindset in relation to supposedly "objective" standards of success. Whose agendas are reflected in those standards? Who is (dis)advantaged or (in/ex)cluded by such standards?
- Decide on your own realistic standards of success that serve your overall goals. Break them down into achievable steps that allow for a sense of accomplishment and success.
- Create a "fact file" (e.g. a collection of positive feedback you've received, or a list of successes and achievements) that you can return to as objective evidence when you experience imposter feelings.
- Find real life examples of imperfect but published/completed work, to show you that it doesn't have to be perfect to get the job done. Katrina remembers reading what seemed like some very poor quality theses as part of her doctoral work, and thinking: "If they got a doctorate for *that*, I'm definitely not giving up!"
- Learn more about imposter syndrome, perfectionism, and their prevalence in academia, to help you recognise the external factors that create these feelings and that have nothing to do with your ability or performance.
- Use journaling, art, or creative writing to explore and re-present your imposter or perfectionist experiences. For example, Hoben et al. (2022) constructed a fairytale and Singh (2022) created a piece of art[1] based on (and to disrupt) their experiences of imposter syndrome.
- Take Brene Brown's (2012) advice and write on a 1-inch square piece of paper the names of the (few) people whose opinions of you actually matter. The 1-inch size ensures this list is small! Keep the list handy and use it to help restore perspective in the face of imposter messages.
- Check whether your institution offers free or subsidised counselling or coaching for students. Talking through

imposter feelings or perfectionism in such an environ-ment can be helpful. Further, imposter/perfectionist feelings can be linked (often without us realising) to past experiences such as trauma that may need to be worked through with a clinical specialist (Dobos et al., 2021).

The distance lens on imposter syndrome and per-fectionism is, as always, not one-dimensional. Some students find being away from campus protects them from the negative effects of constant comparisons with other researchers. This helps reduce imposter feelings, enculturation into potentially unhealthy work cultures, and competitively motivated perfectionism. For others based off-campus, though, the lack of interaction with other doctoral students creates problems: If all we see is other doctoral students' completed, polished, corrected theses and not the many re-writes, edits, and feelings that went into their production, it's easy to think that other students are wonderfully competent and that we are the only ones who struggle. We may also not have such ready access to others who can offer us a more balanced perspective on ourselves or our work. See Chapter 7 for more on how to maintain connections with other researchers at a distance.

Nurturing your health and wellbeing

Doctoral research is meant to be challenging and certainly asks a lot of us, even in ideal circumstances. When we're doing anything ambitious, it's important to be proactive in caring for ourselves across physical, mental, emotional, spiritual, and relational domains in ways that align with our values and priorities.

Unfortunately, some students—including distance students—struggle with maintaining their health and wellbeing during doctoral research. Much research work is sedentary, reducing our levels of physical activity. One recent study found that only 38% of doctoral students engaged in the recommended amounts of physical activity (Ndupu et al., 2023). Physical health, diet, exercise, and sleep are important in their own right as well as for their impacts on our mental health, productivity, and cognitive capacity. Doctoral researchers can experience higher than usual levels of stress, burnout, anxiety, and depression (Ayres, 2022), with mental health among doctoral students worsening over time (Nature Editors, 2019). Engaging in doctoral education may also produce, reproduce, or trigger trauma (McChesney, 2022), complicating doctoral students' ability to engage in knowledge production, navigate institutional and academic landscapes, and speak up when they need support. Further, as with many of the other issues raised in this book, social and demographic characteristics as well as our individual life circumstances intersect with our access to aspects of health and wellbeing.

> **STUDENT VOICE:** "[Challenges for me included] distractions working at home as nobody is there to hold me accountable. I can spend days procrastinating because I have no idea how to tackle a task / seems too hard. Stress eating, poor sleep from there being a blur between personal life and doctoral studies ..."

Importantly, however, there are also many positive stories of doctoral researchers thriving and enjoying positive health and wellbeing (see, for example, Byrom et al., 2022; Winter et al., 2021). It's possible to have a positive, satisfying doctoral journey and, while there are undoubtedly things about higher education systems and environments that need addressing, there are also concrete things you can do that enhance your experience. As the saying goes, *if you don't make time for your health, you'll be forced* (i.e. through illness, injury, or burnout) *to make time for your health.*

Byrom et al.'s (2022) research identified a range of factors that are important for doctoral researchers' stress and mental wellbeing: supervisory support; feeling confidently prepared; confidence regarding career direction(s); family support; avoiding self-depreciation/imposter feelings; an achievement orientation (i.e. "motivation, enthusiasm and preparation for academic work"; p. 785); overall health; and hours of sleep. Likewise, Jackman et al.'s (2022) literature review highlighted concerns about being a doctoral student; doctoral study processes; personal circumstances (e.g. finances, relationships, language difficulties, work-life balance); support networks; scholarly community support; and self-care and lifestyle factors as linked to doctoral student mental health and wellbeing. You might think about these factors as "levers" shaping your experience. Are there some levers that you could adjust to better support your mental health and wellbeing?

It's also worth reviewing some of the basics of health and wellbeing for anyone. The things that help us flourish in other parts of our lives don't stop being relevant just because we're doctoral researchers! We have to be vigilant in fighting for these "basics", as was the case for the women doctoral students who participated in Schmidt and Umans's (2014) study:

> Almost all students stated they were unwilling to compromise their private life for the sake of succeeding in their studies. Yet many of

them admitted that at times when the work-load became heavier and in stressful situations (typically before submitting a paper, middle or final seminars, teaching in combination with research, presentations, or participation in conferences), other parts of their lives suffered and led to feelings of guilt, frustration, and bad conscience. In a few cases, it required a personal crisis before they realized that other parts in their life besides study had to be prioritized for their own well-being. (p. 6)

You might find it beneficial to:

- Connect with nature—go for a walk; look up at the sky or out at the water, garden, or trees; and use your senses to notice the sights, sounds, smells, and textures around you.
- Exercise in a way that you enjoy.
- Review your sleep habits and set alarms to help manage this.
- Eat foods that fuel your body well, and reduce foods that don't.
- Spend time with friends (or seek new friends, if needed) and family.
- Connect with others online.
- Take a break.
- Volunteer, help someone, or give something to others in need.
- Journal.
- Give yourself headspace—step away from the imme-diate task if you know you need time to think, process, settle your emotions, or otherwise be well.

- Practise gratitude, mindfulness, positive thinking and/ or meditation.
- Make time (even a little!) for hobbies and things that give you joy.
- Identify and start to tackle unhelpful habits e.g. procrastination, task avoidance, perfectionism.
- Seek help, whether with difficult aspects of your doctoral work, with the "life stuff" you happen to be dealing with, or with your health and/or wellbeing.
- Build in regular times and practices that help you reflect on your health and wellbeing, such as journaling or checking in with a coach, counsellor, or accountability partner.

> **STUDENT VOICE:** "Celebrate EVERYTHING. Every chapter draft, every conference abstract submission, every decent review. Every time you have the opportunity, celebrate. And rest."

Considering how you might take action around your health and wellbeing on top of the demands of the doctorate can feel overwhelming. Give yourself permission to be on the journey (a process orientation), rather than expecting yourself to have "arrived" in some perfectly disciplined, balanced, healthy and well life (a goal orientation). What matters most is that you are intentionally journeying toward health and wellbeing rather than simply ignoring or sacrificing these aspects of your life. Remember, too, that balance often happens over time, not in each individual day or week.

If you find yourself struggling with your mental health and wellbeing, do seek support. You might start by seeing your GP; talking to a counsellor, coach, or advisor from your university; or diving into texts such as Petra Boynton's (2021) *Being Well in Academia: Ways to feel Stronger, Safer, and More Connected*; Zoe Ayres's (2022) *Managing your Mental Health during your PhD: A Survival Guide*, or Narelle Lemon's edited series on *Wellbeing and Self-care in Higher Education.*[2]

If necessary, you could suspend your doctoral enrolment to allow you time to deal with any health-related challenges, including mental health. Rest assured, you will not be the first student your graduate school or supervisor has encountered who needs to do this. There should be procedures and options that you can consider, and you are entitled to respect, responsiveness, and support in the process. If any of these are not forthcoming, seek allies such as your supervisors or student association representatives in negotiating a pathway that will allow you to be healthy and well so that you can complete your studies. The advice in Chapter 8 will also be of use in these circumstances.

> **STUDENT VOICE:** "My (already diagnosed) anxiety and depression were much worse during the pandemic, and I realised I needed further professional help in order to maintain my studies. I regularly saw (online) a psychologist and started medication. This helped me reduce my worrying and re-focus on my studies."

Ultimately, your health and wellbeing are important investments in yourself for their own sake AND help equip you to be able to do your best scholarly work. Don't shortchange yourself by cutting out time for these things in order to meet your academic, family, employment, or community commitments; this may work in the short term but, in the longer term, it will undermine your wellbeing and ability to progress.

> **STUDENT VOICE:** "[As a distance student] I was able to focus more on my health and find out what type of working environment I thrived in. Being able to set my own hours (as no commute or parking woes existed) meant that I found I worked better by starting later, and did not need to "work" for as long, as I was more productive after having a good night's sleep and waking up when it was natural."

Activity: Automatic thoughts

This cognitive behavioural therapy technique focuses on identifying and then disrupting our automatic thoughts—"the thoughts that automatically arise in our minds all throughout the day" (Bonfil & Wagage, 2020). Our assumptions and default patterns of thinking drive our feelings and behaviour:

> Automatic thoughts have the potential to trigger intense negative emotions. Usually, we are more aware of the emotions themselves than the thoughts that trigger them. However, in most instances *it is the automatic thoughts that play the largest role in determining how we feel, not the situation itself*. Learning to examine these thoughts allows us to better understand and deal with our emotions, modulating them before they get too intense or overwhelming. (Bonfil & Wagage, 2020, our emphasis)

We can train ourselves to notice our automatic negative thoughts and evaluate whether they are really accurate or supporting the kinds of feelings and behaviours we want for ourselves. Luckily, as a doctoral student, your thinking and metacognition (thinking about your thinking) skills are already in excellent shape, positioning you well for such self-examination!

Below are some examples of automatic negative thoughts related to the issues explored in this chapter, and some more positive (and likely more truthful) reframings. Which ones resonate with you? What other automatic negative thoughts do you fall victim to? Try writing down your own most common automatic thoughts and what you see as more positive mindset alternatives for each one.

Automatic thought: I don't really belong here/I'm not as good as the other doctoral students/people are looking down on me or judging me for not being good enough.

- Everyone here feels nervous and unsure—it's the nature of academic environments and doing something as stretchy and complex as a doctoral degree.

Automatic thought: This work is really hard and feels uncomfortable. I want to avoid it/hide from my supervisor(s)/pretend to be busy by doing lots of (not really necessary) reading/organising/note making/list making etc.

- I chose to do this challenging, ambitious, exciting, messy thing (a doctorate) because I love my field, am passionate about my topic, and like learning new things. I can show up for myself even when it's hard, and I know that "not knowing" is a normal part of the process.

Automatic thought: Being a distance student/juggling my kids/work/care responsibilities alongside my distance study/living away from campus (etc) means I'm a burden or an outsider in terms of the university/how my supervisor(s) like(s) to work/being able to access support at my institution, and this is just something I have to deal with.

• I'm on this path for a reason, and it's great to be able to do my doctorate while living where I live/balancing my other commitments and the things that are important to me. I am entitled to be supported as well as any other student at my institution, and I can speak up to try and make things better.

Automatic thought: I don't have time to exercise/meditate/cook nutritious meals—that all has to be parked until I get this doctorate completed.

• By looking after my body and mind, I'm investing in my ability to do my doctoral work well and make it out the other side in healthy ways.

Notes

1 *Lizard Person*; used as the cover image of the *Palgrave Handbook of Imposter Syndrome in Higher Education*.
2 See www.routledge.com/Wellbeing-and-Self-care-in-Higher-Educat ion/book-series/WSCHE

References

Addison, M., Breeze, M., & Taylor, Y. (2022). *The Palgrave handbook of imposter syndrome in higher education.* Palgrave Macmillan.

Ayres, Z. (2022). *Managing your mental health during your PhD: A survival guide.* Springer.

Barnacle, R., & Mewburn, I. (2010). Learning networks and the journey of 'becoming doctor'. *Studies in Higher Education, 35*(4), 433–444. https://doi.org/10.1080/03075070903131214

Bitzer, E., & van den Bergh, S. (2014). Doctoral identity change towards researcher autonomy during research journeys across disciplines. *South African Journal of Higher Education, 28*(3), 1047–1068.

Bonfil, A., & Wagage, S. (2020). *A course in CBT techniques: A free online CBT workbook.* Cognitive Behavioral Therapy Los Angeles. https://cogbtherapy.com/free-online-cbt-workbook

Boynton, P. (2021). *Being well in academia: Ways to feel stronger, safer, and more connected.* Routledge.

Brown, B. (2012). *Daring greatly.* Penguin Random House.

Byrom, N. C., Dinu, L., Kirkman, A., & Hughes, G. (2022). Predicting stress and mental wellbeing among doctoral researchers. *Journal of Mental Health, 31*(6), 783–791. https://doi.org/10.1080/09638237.2020.1818196

Carvalho, L., & Freeman, C. (2022). Materials and places for learning: Experiences of doctoral students in and around university spaces. *Postdigital Science and Education.* https://doi.org/10.1007/s42438-022-00328-x

Chakraverty, D. (2020). PhD student experiences with the imposter phenomenon in STEM. *International Journal of Doctoral Studies, 15,* 159–179. https://doi.org/10.28945/4513

Dobos, B., Piko, B. F., & Mellor, D. (2021). What makes university students perfectionists? The role of childhood trauma, emotional dysregulation, academic anxiety and social support. *Scandinavian Journal of Psychology.* https://doi.org/10.1111/sjop.12718

Hoben, J., Badenhorst, C., & Pickett, S. (2022). Sprinting in glass slippers: Fairy tales as resistance to imposter syndrome in academia. In Addison, M., Breeze, M., & Taylor, Y. (Eds.). *The Palgrave handbook of imposter syndrome in higher education* (pp. 211–224). Palgrave Macmillan.

Jackman, P., Jacobs, L., Hawkins, R. M., & Sisson, K. (2022). Mental health and psychological wellbeing in the early stages of doctoral study: A systematic review. *European Journal of Higher Education, 12*(3), 293–313. https://doi.org/10.1080/21568235.2021.1939752

Kamler, B., & Thomson, P. (2014). *Helping doctoral students write: Pedagogies for supervision* (2nd ed.). Routledge.

Kearns, H. (2015). *The imposter syndrome: Why successful people often feel like frauds.* ThinkWell.

Kearns, H., & Gardiner, M. (2009). *Defeating self-sabotage: Getting your PhD finished.* ThinkWell.

Leach, E. (2021). The fractured "I": An autoethnographic account of a part-time doctoral student's experience with scholarly identity formation. *Qualitative Inquiry*, *27*(3–4), 381–384. https://doi.org/10.1177/1077800420918895

Mantai, L. (2017). Feeling like a researcher: Experiences of early doctoral students in Australia. *Studies in Higher Education*, *42*(4), 636–650. https://doi.org/10.1080/03075079.2015.1067603

McAlpine, L. (2012). Identity-trajectories: Doctoral journeys from past to present to future. *Australian Universities' Review*, *54*(1), 39–46.

McAlpine, L., Amundsen, C., & Turner, G. (2014). Identity-trajectory: Reframing early career academic experience. *British Educational Research Journal*, *40*(6), 952–969. https://doi.org/10.1002/berj.3123

McChesney, K. (2022). A rationale for trauma-informed postgraduate supervision. *Teaching in Higher Education: Critical Perspectives.* https://doi.org/10.1080/13562517.2022.2145469

Nature Editors. (2019). The mental health of PhD researchers demands urgent attention [editorial]. *Nature*, *575*, 257–258. https://doi.org/10.1038/d41586-019-03489-1

Ndupu, L. B., Faghy, M., Staples, V., Lipka, S., & Bussell, C. (2023). Exploring the predictors of physical inactivity in a university setting. *BMC Public Health*, *23*, 59. https://doi.org/10.1186/s12889-022-14953-5

Schmidt, M., & Umans, T. (2014). Experiences of well-being among female doctoral students in Sweden. *International Journal of Qualitative Studies on Health and Well-being*, *9*, 23059. https://doi.org/10.3402/qhw.v9.23059

Singh, S. (2022). Peeling away imposterism. In M. Addison, M. Breeze, & Y. Taylor (Eds.). *The Palgrave handbook of imposter syndrome in higher education* (pp. v–ix). Palgrave Macmillan.

Winter, T., Riordan, B. C., Hunter, J. A., Tustin, K., Gollop, M., Taylor, N., Kokaua, J., Poulton, R., & Scarf, D. (2021). A longitudinal study of mental wellbeing in students in Aotearoa New Zealand who transitioned into PhD study. *Frontiers in Psychology*, *12*, 659163. https://doi.org/10.3389/fpsyg.2021.659163

6 Supervision work

Communicating, learning, and connecting via distance

Around the world and across disciplines, doctoral researchers are supported, mentored, and overseen by one or more academic staff. These staff may be referred to as supervisors, advisors, guides, or committee members, and the exact definitions of their roles can vary. For simplicity, we refer to them all as "supervisors" throughout this book. Your ongoing relationship with these key people will be a defining characteristic of your doctoral experience. This chapter considers four ways you can help make your supervision experience as positive as possible: (i) understanding the nature and purpose of supervision; (ii) starting well by developing a positive supervisory relationship, (iii) working productively with your supervisors via distance, and (iv) cultivating shared understanding between students and supervisors.

> **STUDENT VOICE:** "The most important factor in being a distance student is maintaining a good relationship with a patient, supportive supervisor."

DOI: 10.4324/9781003334088-6

Understanding the purpose and nature of supervision

Doctoral supervision was historically built on a hierarchical master-apprentice model, but nowadays a wider range of relationship styles might be established to support doctoral researchers' developing identity, creativity, and independence. As a doctoral researcher, you're not a passive recipient of knowledge and skills—you're an active participant in the knowledge creation process alongside your supervisor(s). Your supervisor(s) are not there to teach you everything that you need to know, and they are not in sole control of how supervision will look (although they will almost certainly have some views on this!).

Supervision can take a range of forms. There are usually basic official expectations for supervision, which may be defined for specific programmes of study or institution-wide. These provide a starting point and can help you calibrate your expectations and flag issues if you're not sure whether you are receiving adequate supervision. Beyond these, however, there's no single, correct way for the supervisory relationship to be—it depends very much on the field of study, your cultural and/or institutional context, and the personalities involved. For example, in some disciplines it's common to work in labs or research groups, and you might work alongside your supervisor(s) closely as you learn to use equipment or software, conduct experiments, or undertake a large piece of collaborative fieldwork. In other disciplines, you might see your supervisor(s) less frequently (e.g. once a month) and not be connected to your supervisor's other research students. Regardless of discipline, doctoral students' motivations and personalities might inform what they want to get out of doctoral supervision and how they approach it. Supervisors also bring their own personalities, beliefs, and approaches to supervision, which may or may not match what you would prefer!

The focuses of supervision interactions can change over time. At different stages of your research, your interactions with supervisors may centre around discussing literature, methodology, data collection or analysis, your written drafts, or problems that have arisen along the way. You might collectively engage in debate, test-drive or unpack challenging ideas, or ruminate together on questions—including questions the supervisor(s) don't know the answer to! Most supervisors will try to ask questions to get you talking and stretch your thinking further. As your project unfolds, be aware that situations and expectations can change, relational dynamics can shift, and disagreements may arise—even in highly productive and supportive supervisory teams.

Crucially, much of the learning depends on you. As a doctoral student you are very much in the driver's seat, with your supervisors being experienced travellers coming along for the ride (McChesney, 2023). Distance doctoral researchers and their supervisors can be thought of as a community of geographically distributed peers (Huijser et al., 2022), rather than as teachers and a learner.

In the wake of the COVID-19 pandemic, many supervisors have learned to become more flexible in working with students at a distance (Wisker et al., 2021), with some supervisors even welcoming the conditions that digital technologies enable. Regardless of how comfortable your supervisors may initially be with distance modes, supervision is something that is always negotiated (Frick et al., 2014). Therefore, we invite you to imagine yourself as a key participant in shaping the kind of supervision you experience. This chapter aims to help you recognise the things you can do to encourage the kind of supervisory interactions that are most effective in facilitating your learning, growth, and—ultimately—successful doctoral completion.

Starting well: Establishing a positive supervisory relationship at a distance

Supervisors act as the primary source of support for most doctoral researchers, so it's important to try and establish a strong relationship. Start well by aiming to establish strong bonds early, and then make the effort to maintain these across the supervision relationship. Doing this can help prevent miscommunication, confusion, and conflict.

> **STUDENT VOICE:** "Find ways to make a personal connection with your supervisor at the start."

Building any relationship requires time spent getting to know each other in a context of mutual respect, engagement, and genuine interest. If you're able to make it into campus even once to have a coffee or lunch in person with your supervisor, this less-formal time together can be a great launch for an ongoing distance relationship. Show an interest in your supervisor's research, background, family (if appropriate in your cultural context), and other research students. Ask if you can be put in contact with those other students. Share some things about yourself, too, to the level that you feel comfortable, and note any things you find you have in common—relationships are built on these points of connection and shared knowledge. And do take the time to learn to pronounce your supervisor's name correctly, especially if it's from a language or culture you're not used to!

> **STUDENT VOICE:** "If possible, meet your supervisor, cohort, and department in person, preferably at the beginning of the doctorate. It's easier to form those relationships in person and then move to distance."

Cultural differences (Nasiri & Mafakheri, 2015), being a first-generation student (Gardner & Holley, 2011), or a background of physical or mental health challenges or even trauma (McChesney, 2022) can influence interaction between you and your supervisor(s). Disclosing personal challenges can be a double-edged sword, and you'll have to gauge what you feel comfortable with sharing at each stage of your journey. However, you can overcome many challenges related to differing worldviews or experiences through a combination of reciprocal relationship building, effective delegation of tasks, and remaining adaptable (Huijser et al., 2022)—proactive strategies that form the principles of building positive distance supervisory relationships. If you think that specific things such as a disability, a language barrier, or your personal circumstances are likely to affect your doctoral work, it would be wise to have an open conversation with your supervisor(s) about this as early as you feel comfortable. Supervisors can't help if they aren't aware of what you're experiencing, and it may be easier to have an open conversation before challenges arise.

It can be useful to clarify the expectations around supervision that you and your supervisor(s) hold. This should begin early in the supervision process and can be renegotiated as your research progresses. The activity at the end of this chapter highlights tools you can use to help you understand and negotiate supervisory expectations, and you may even develop a written memorandum of understanding with your supervisor(s). Many universities require such agreements as part of their formal processes to help ensure that supervision relationships start out with clear, shared understanding on key issues. Whether formalised in writing or not, some key questions to ask yourself and discuss with your supervisor(s) include big picture things (e.g. who sets the objectives or methodology for your project? How are issues of authorship and intellectual property negotiated?), as well as small but significant things around the practicalities of your meetings (e.g. where/when will you meet? Who sets the agenda for a supervision session? Who keeps track of deadlines? What's the timeframe required to send and receive feedback on writing?). And if you do happen to be located somewhere that would make it possible for you to go to campus sometimes, explicitly discuss what mode(s) of supervision (ranging between fully online and fully in-person) might suit you and your supervisor(s) best.

STUDENT VOICES: "Set up clear expectations with your supervisor and collaborators from the start regarding communication preferences—how do they prefer to be contacted? When and how often? Are there specific platforms/days/times that don't work for them?"

It can be helpful in this process to reflect on what factors are shaping your expectations of supervision. Are you bringing professional conventions or your life experience into the mix? Have you been supervised before, and might you be anticipating something similar? How do you know that what you're expecting is realistic, appropriate at doctoral level, or aligned with your supervisor's work-load and the institution's expectations for supervision?

Another thing that's important to establish in your supervisory relationship is trust (Robertson, 2017). Trust grows as you let your supervisor "in" on your thinking, questions, struggles, and ideas-in-progress, as well as when you deliver what you have said you will, show that you are making genuine use of your supervisors' feedback, and continue to remain present rather than withdrawing or "hiding" when things get tough. These are all things you can do at a distance. Developing trust takes time and feeling emotionally and intellectually safe, so don't expect it to happen overnight. But without trust, it is more difficult to overcome the inevitable tensions that can occur along the doctoral journey, potentially jeopardising the quality or progress of your work.

Working productively with your supervisor(s) at a distance

Distance doesn't have to be an obstacle to productive doctoral supervision. Many of the core functions of doc-toral supervision (e.g. thinking and discussing together, giving/receiving feedback) can happen effectively via video meetings or other modes of connection. Distance supervision through online-enabled mediums can actu-ally improve supervision frequency, flexibility, diversity and access (Kumar et al., 2020). The key is to be aware of the key elements of effective supervision (regular con-tact, purposeful engagement, a balance between flexi-bility and accountability, feedback, and a well-functioning team) and work out how you can address these elements in ways that work for you and your supervisors. There are lots of possibilities, and we discuss each element below.

> **STUDENT VOICES:** "Ideally I would like to have a hybrid way of working mostly from a distance and then meeting face-to-face over 3-5 days once a semester or even once a year."

Having **regular contact** with your supervisor(s) is important for maintaining timely, open, and consistent interaction. In our survey of over 500 distance doctoral researchers, online video conferencing platforms (such as Zoom or Microsoft Teams) and email were the most common ways students kept in contact with their supervisors. Other kinds of contact (e.g. telephone, instant messaging, and travelling to meet their supervisors in person) were also used, although less commonly. Do discuss what modes of communication might work for you and your supervisor. Depending on personality and cultural contexts, supervisors may have strong views around what modes of communication are appropriate for these exchanges. For example, some may be horrified at the idea of a text or WhatsApp message from a student, while others may welcome this approach. It's good to find out beforehand what would work!

> **STUDENT VOICE:** "Having worked out ways of being in touch with my supervisors—and scheduling these on a rolling basis—has helped me feel connected. We pre-plan our meetings at the start of each year, and book in the Zoom sessions. It helps enormously."

Face-to-face time talking with your supervisors can be incredibly powerful. If possible, schedule regular meetings with your supervisor(s), whether in person or online. Depending on the stage your research is at and your institution's guidelines, these meetings may occur weekly, fortnightly, or monthly. Scheduled supervision appointments support continued progress (more frequent supervision is associated with timely completion; Pyhältö et al., 2015) and ensure you have your supervisor(s)' attention on a regular basis. Be proactive around scheduling these meetings—remember, you are in the driver's seat, so don't just wait for your supervisor to reach out to you. And if your supervisor(s) have regular virtual office hours that work for you, these can be a great additional way to stay connected. You'll meet other students who drop in and can discuss quick or immediate questions rather than waiting for the next formal supervision.

> **STUDENT VOICE:** "My supervisor runs monthly catch-up Zoom sessions for aligned researchers in our department. So, on a monthly basis, we like-minded graduate researchers chat about what we've been doing, interesting papers/resources that we've come across, etc. It helps widen our connectivity, and helps to cement our connection to our university, our department, and our field of study."

The most effective supervision meetings are ***purposeful***, using time well and remaining focused on the most important things. Try sending your supervisor(s) a clear agenda before each meeting that details the points you would like to discuss (see Kearns & Gardiner, 2012, for more on this). Katrina also has her research students send through an update on what they've done since the last meeting, what they've been accessing to support their learning, and how they are feeling in terms of progress, the project, and wellbeing. Written updates like this and focused meeting agendas make it easier for your supervisor(s) to catch up on what you've been doing and allow everyone to focus on the most important topics or questions in your precious face-to-face meeting time. These practices also demonstrate your commitment and independence, fuelling supervisors' trust in your professional judgement. To ensure you stay on track, it is useful to take notes during the meeting and share these with your supervisor(s) afterwards so that everyone can check and agree upon what was discussed and the next steps. Recording supervision meetings (with everyone's consent) can also allow you to revisit details and advice you might have missed.

Because you're doing something unpredictable (independent research) within fixed time constraints (your doctoral enrolment), supervision needs a balance of ***flexibility and accountability***. Regular supervision meetings where you provide updates on your progress keep you accountable, as do agreed deadlines for when you are going to send your supervisors a particular piece of writing or analysis. If your supervisors know and trust you, however, they will be understanding and supportive if "life happens" and things sometimes do not go as planned (see also Chapter 8). Keeping a close eye on your plans and timelines (see Chapter 2) and updating these as the project unfolds can help you balance ongoing flexibility with ensuring you and your supervisors can feel confident that the work is indeed going to be completed in the required timeframe.

Another area where you may need flexibility is around modes of communication. You'll have patterns and normal ways of working, but when one mode of communication does not suffice, try another. For example, if you're really stuck or do not understand some written feedback, you could request a video call or an in-person meeting (if you're close enough to campus for this to be possible) to facilitate clarification. It's helpful to communicate the purpose of the additional meeting request clearly so your supervisor(s) can come prepared.

> **STUDENT VOICE:** "Use online and in person meetings to their own advantages. Cherish the flexibility and freedom of online. Equally treasure in-person moments."

Supervisors should provide timely and relevant *feedback* on doctoral work, although they can only do so when they have something concrete on which to comment. Written evidence of your progress can range from short updates that can be reviewed quickly to more substantive pieces of written work (e.g. draft chapters) that require longer review times. If a supervision meeting will centre on discussing your draft work, be respectful of your supervisors' time by ensuring you send the relevant drafts in a timely manner prior to the meeting (e.g. one week for a shorter piece, longer for a longer piece). Remember that quality formative feedback takes significant time to construct and that supervisors have lots of other tasks and deadlines to juggle.

There are a variety of ways supervisors can provide formative feedback to distance doctoral researchers, spanning written/spoken and synchronous/asynchronous communication (Nasiri & Mafakheri, 2015; Wisker et al., 2021). Even though you and your supervisor(s) may have particular preferences when it comes to receiving and providing feedback, there is no one-size-fits-all approach. Your need to receive feedback needs to be balanced with your supervisor(s)' workload and commitments. Discuss your feedback needs and preferences (including focus, depth, timing, and mode of communication) openly with your supervisor(s). You could also point out areas that you would like comments on and any questions you have for your supervisors as they review a particular draft.

In many contexts, **co- and team supervision approaches** are becoming more commonplace. These protect doctoral researchers from being reliant on only one supervisor as their sole source of information and support. The COVID-19 pandemic has facilitated the emergence of better cross-national and team-based ways of supervising distance doctoral researchers (Stevens et al., 2021). However, team-based supervision can be more difficult to sustain online than one-to-one supervision (Torka, 2021). Try to ensure group meetings are accessible and suitable to everyone involved, e.g. by considering any time zone differences, each person's availability, internet connectivity, and preferred ways of working. At times, you may agree together to intersperse team meetings with individual meetings, such as if roles and responsibilities are being shared out among the different team members (perhaps with one supervisor overseeing the methodology but another overseeing the literature work). If you have individual meetings, remember to keep the whole team up to date to avoid confusion or conflict.

Digital tools to support distance supervision

Digital tools can be great enablers for online and remote ways of working, provided you have the necessary internet access and hardware. Video conferencing platforms (such as Microsoft Teams, Zoom, and Skype) enable many distance doctoral researchers and their supervisors to communicate virtually almost as if everyone were sitting around the same table (Torka, 2021). Cloud-based tools and instant chat apps (such Microsoft Teams, Google Drive, and Slack) are useful ways to store, share, discuss, and collaborate on materials with your supervisor(s), both synchronously and asynchronously. Shared documents foster shared ownership, keep version control on your radar, and ensure your work is always backed up. There are also a multitude of free online tools for sharing work and brainstorming (e.g. Wondershare Edrawmind, Miro or Zoom whiteboards, Stormboard, Inspiration, Mural, and Trello). Screen-sharing tools and collaborative documents allow supervisors and distance doctoral researchers to literally be "on the same page, at the same time", bridging the separation in time and/or space that distance students can experience. Finally, AI transcription tools such as Otter can be used to create live transcripts from supervision meetings for easy reference afterwards. Chances are, you may work with a combination of platforms and tools across your doctoral journey. Don't be afraid to experiment with new ways of working online!

STUDENT VOICE: "Being able to take digital notes, look up information and share links during meetings made for a richer collaboration. Using tools like Jamboard for collaboration allowed the artifacts of collaboration to live beyond the moment."

It is important not to romanticise online ways of working. They don't just tidy up all the power relations involved in supervision, for example, and some tools may be more or less accessible for students with disabilities, learning differences, or financial constraints. However, there can be lots to like about them from the student's perspective. Jamie, for example, remembers nervously waiting outside his supervisor's office the few times he had supervision face-to-face on campus. Somehow, this wait conjured up feelings of the student waiting to go into the principal's office! In contrast, when Jamie met his supervisors from the comfort of home via video call, the dynamics of supervision were able to be negotiated differently, particularly those that take place when bodies mingle in person (e.g. how do we greet each other? Who sits in what chair, and what do these positions signify?). Often, Jamie and his supervisors were all beamed into each other's houses, with real life taking place in the background. This experience mirrors many forms of research collaboration in academic life which are mediated by digital tools, including the way we as a team of four (some of whom have never met in person) wrote this book! In this sense, perhaps distance communication with supervisors provides quite good preparation for future digital-savvy collaboration work.

Digital tools can be particularly empowering for certain groups of students. For example, for students with disabilities or learning differences, being able to record and review supervision meetings, pausing and replaying as needed, removes the pressure to absorb everything "in the moment". Turning on automated captioning during video meetings can also greatly help non-native English students or those with hearing difficulties or auditory processing disorder.

Interpersonal communication can be different in online spaces, and people will have different levels of comfort and literacy with particular technologies. Some people might become more self-conscious and less spontaneous when interacting online. Video meetings often involve more direct eye contact but less ability to read body language. Humour may not transfer as well on screen, and more attention may need to be paid to turn-taking in online conversations so everyone feels they have given input and been heard/seen. Gaining familiarity with the team and the technology, however, usually smooths interactions, and bringing in some additional tools (such as the examples above) may help complement your video interactions and enhance everyone's engagement and understanding.

While there are lots of great digital tools available, we recognise that the playing field is not equal for distance doctoral researchers in remote areas, in financial hardship, or where there is limited internet connectivity. Thus, when selecting tools, you'll need to consider your own and your supervisor(s)' access to computer hardware and software, your bandwidth and connectivity, and everyone's skill (and willingness) in using different communication platforms. If you're struggling to cover the costs of digital devices or internet service, ask if your university offers student hardship support or relevant scholarships that could help.

Ultimately, whatever your distance situation looks like, it's important to work to find communication modes that suit everyone involved and facilitate effective connections between you and your supervisor(s). Proactively considering the tools and platforms that might work for you and your supervisors is just another element of seeing supervision as a "negotiated learning space" (Frick et al., 2014, p. 241).

Cultivating shared understanding across contexts

Some distance doctoral researchers' fieldwork happens in contexts that are relatively familiar to supervisors. Perhaps the research sites might be schools, businesses, or natural spaces in similar geographic and cultural contexts as the university. However, other doctoral research takes place beyond supervisors' immediate environments—perhaps overseas, or perhaps in a highly specific context that supervisors have not previously entered (e.g. a specialist healthcare or corrections setting). Alternatively, you yourself may be located in a different country context that's very different from your supervisor's location. In such cases, it can be useful to help your supervisor(s) build an understanding of your home and/or research contexts so that the feedback they offer can be most constructive for you.

The distance doctoral education literature provides some lovely examples of how this shared understanding can be developed, noting the benefits of investing in this work. For example, Huijser et al. (2022) show how distance doctoral researcher Sazan Mandalawi was able to acquaint her supervisory team in Australia with her study context, a refugee camp in Iraq. Likewise, Zondi Mkhabela and Liezel (author) have written about how their relationship across both distance and cultural divides helped them to become better scholars through learning to understand each other's contexts, building mutual kindness and trust, agreeing not to compromise on quality, and making use of other experts when appropriate (Mkhabela & Frick, 2016).

We suggest you start by finding out how much (if any) exposure your supervisor(s) have had to your home and/or research contexts. If the answer is "not much", how can you help them learn about those environments? What is important for them to understand? It may even be possible for your supervisor(s) to visit you or your study site at some stage, perhaps by identifying a conference that is occurring nearby and planning a combined trip. Whatever the method, building mutual understanding and respect around your unique context will enable your supervisor(s) to advise you with insight and contextual sensitivity. The time spent helping your supervisor(s) understand the nuances of your context may also be useful when it comes to writing up your thesis, as you'll realise what things need to be made explicit to support readers unfamiliar with your research context.

If supervision breaks down

Sometimes supervision relationships do break down, for a variety of reasons. Indicators include the supervisor simply not being available, communicating with you, or providing feedback on your work over an extended period (recognising that everyone has peaks and troughs in their workload and that supervisors can take sick leave and annual leave too). More subtle indications can be found in your own feelings, such as if you are finding yourself dreading or avoiding supervision and/or feeling like you can't open up and share how you are really feeling (in relation to the project and your learning journey — remembering that they are not your counsellor!) or what questions you are struggling to resolve. It's never nice having to work through these issues or change supervisors, but if you find yourself in this sort of situation it is better to take action than to either abandon your doctorate or try to "go it alone" (complete the doctorate without engaging with your supervisor/s).

If things are not working well, it's a good idea to address concerns you have with your supervisor(s) directly first if you can. Was there a mix-up because information is missing or a process hasn't been followed? Is something going wrong on a personal level (e.g. illness or a bereavement) on either side? Have expectations been mis-communicated?

If the situation does not seem easily resolved, it's important to know what avenues are available to you to raise your concerns. Usually, universities have formalised processes and procedures in place to support you in considering the best way to resolve conflict. These processes may include you talking to a leader in your academic department, seeking support from a staff member at a doctoral college, or having a mediated discussion (e.g. with an advocate or representative of a student union present). Hopefully, you'll never need to use these processes, but it's good to know they're there and how to access them.

Activity: Supervision scaffolds

A number of tools have been developed to help doctoral researchers and their supervisors establish positive ways of working and/or reflect on their established interactions. Such tools can be:

- helpful scaffolds early in your doctorate, getting unspoken expectations out into the open and inviting agreement on ways of working;
- used or revisited when key milestones (e.g. confirmation, upgrade, annual progress reviews) roll around; or
- a "way in" to discussing how things are going if things aren't feeling quite right.

Look at one or more of the tools below. Consider whether it might be a useful scaffold for a conversation with your supervisor.

- The *Feedback Expectation Tool* (FET), available in the Appendix to Stracke and Kumar (2020)
- *Supervisory Expectations Checklist*, available in Appendix 1 of Carter et al. (2016)
- *Expectations of Research Supervisors*, available online at www.ithinkwell.com.au/index.php?route=product/product/freedownload&download_id=37

References

Carter, S., Laurs, D., Chant, L., Higgins, R., Martin, J., Teaiwa, T., & Wolfgramm-Foliaki, E. (2016). *A guide for supervisors: Supporting doctoral writing: He ara tika mā ngā kaiārahi.* https://ako.ac.nz/assets/Knowledge-centre/rhpf-N66-Giving-feedback-on-doctoral-writing/GUIDE-A-Guide-for-Supervisors-Supporting-Doctoral-Writing-He-Ara-Tika-Ma-Nga-Kaiarahi.pdf

Frick, L., Brodin, E. M., & Albertyn, R. M. (2014). The doctoral student–supervisor relationship as a negotiated learning space. In Scott-Webber, L., Branch, J., Bartholomew, P., & Nygaard, C. (Eds.). *Learning space design in higher education* (pp. 241–262). Libri.

Gardner, S. K., & Holley, K. A. (2011). "Those invisible barriers are real": The progression of first-generation students through doctoral education. *Equity & Excellence in Education*, *44*(1), 77–92. https://doi.org/10.1080/10665684.2011.529791

Huijser, H., Mandalawi, S. M., Henderson, R., & Kek, M. Y. C. A. (2022). Finding a stable core in supervision from a distance: A Kurdish-Australian case study. *Innovations in Education and Teaching International*, *59*(2), 121–130. https://doi.org/10.1080/14703297.2022.2037451

Kearns, H., & Gardiner, M. (2012). *The seven secrets of highly successful research students.* ThinkWell.

Kumar, S., Kumar, V., & Taylor, S. (2020). *A guide to online supervision.* UK Council for Graduate Education. https://supervision.ukcge.ac.uk/cms/wp-content/uploads/A-Guide-to-Online-Supervision-Kumar-Kumar-Taylor-UK-Council-for-Graduate-Education.pdf

McChesney, K. (2022). A rationale for trauma-informed postgraduate supervision. *Teaching in Higher Education: Critical Perspectives.* https://doi.org/10.1080/13562517.2022.2145469

McChesney, K. (2023). Taking the driver's seat in your research journey: Making the most of supervision and professional learning. In Meyer, F. & Meissel, K. (Eds.). *Research methods for education and the social disciplines in Aotearoa New Zealand* (pp. 181–193). NZCER Press.

Mkhabela, Z. L., & Frick, B. L. (2016). Student-supervisor relationships in a complex society: A dual narrative of scholarly becoming. In Frick, B. L., McMaster, C., Murphy, C., & Motshoane, P. (Eds.). *Postgraduate study in South Africa: Surviving and succeeding* (pp. 23–36). African SunMedia.

Nasiri, F., & Mafakheri, F. (2015). Postgraduate research supervision at a distance: a review of challenges and strategies. *Studies in Higher Education*, *40*(10), 1962–1969. https://doi.org/10.1080/03075 079.2014.914906

Pyhältö, K., Vekkaila, J., & Keskinen, J. (2015). Fit matters in the supervisory relationship: Doctoral students and supervisors perceptions about the supervisory activities. *Innovations in Education and Teaching International*, *52*(1), 4–16. https://doi.org/10.1080/14703 297.2014.981836

Robertson, M. J. (2017). Trust: The power that binds in team supervision of doctoral students. *Higher Education Research & Development*, *36*(7), 1463–1475. https://doi.org/10.1080/07294360.2017.1325853

Stevens, D. D., Chetty, R., Bertrand Jones, T., Yallew, A., & Butler-Henderson, K. (2021). Doctoral supervision and COVID-19: Autoethnographies from four faculty across three continents. *Journal of University Teaching & Learning Practice*, *18*(5). https://doi.org/10.53761/1.18.5.6

Stracke, E., & Kumar, V. (2020). Encouraging dialogue in doctoral supervision: The development of the Feedback Expectation Tool. *International Journal of Doctoral Studies*, *15*(1), 265–284. https://doi.org/10.28945/4568

Torka, M. (2021). The transition from in-person to online supervision: Does the interaction between doctoral advisors and candidates change? *Innovations in Education and Teaching International*, *58*(6), 659–671. https://doi.org/10.1080/14703297.2021.1993959

Wisker, G., McGinn, M. K., Bengtsen, S. S. E., Lokhtina, I., He, F., Cornér, S., Leshem, S., Inouye, K., & Löfström, E. (2021). Remote doctoral supervision experiences: Challenges and affordances. *Innovations in Education and Teaching International*, *58*(6), 612–623. https://doi.org/10.1080/14703297.2021.1991427

7 Connection work

Accessing research culture, development, and support communities at a distance

While a doctoral project, by definition, is an independent piece of research, doctoral researchers nonetheless exist within a wider research ecosystem—and this ecosystem can have significant influence on doctoral experiences and outcomes. As a living, growing researcher, you need things that "feed" you and help you flourish. Other people, communities, and events can offer these contributions, provided you are receptive and willing to engage. On the other hand, toxic influences from the research environment that surrounds you can harm and impede your progress, as can a lack of connection to healthy research cultures and communities. Further, while the doctorate can press you to continually gaze inward towards yourself and your own research progress, it is useful to consider how your presence and actions (or lack thereof) within the research ecosystem might influence the experiences of others.

There are many ways to ensure you have a rich and positive experience of research culture and community while undertaking a distance doctorate. In relation to distance doctoral researchers, this chapter addresses: (i) understanding why research culture and communities are important, (ii) examples of specific activities that contribute to stronger research cultures, learning, and communities,

DOI: 10.4324/9781003334088-7

(iii) practical nurturing for support networks, and (iv) the pros and cons of advocacy and self-organising.

STUDENT VOICE: "I thought, when I started this doctoral journey, that it would be about researching and writing, and it would be mostly a solitary endeavour. Instead, I've discovered that it is about sharing, community and connection—and that my community (which is actually often discipline-agnostic) is the secret to moving forward."

Why are research culture and communities important, and why do you need them?

First things first: What is research culture? The UK's Royal Society (n.d.) describes it this way:

> Research culture encompasses the behaviours, values, expectations, attitudes and norms of our research communities. It influences researchers' career paths and determines the way that research is conducted and communicated.

This definition signals that research culture involves certain understood—and acceptable—forms of behaviour that may be dependent on local cultural norms and expectations. As with any culture, there can be positive and negative elements, and even a single institution will have varying research cultures both across and within its schools and departments.

A study of UK researchers' views about their surrounding research cultures found that "78% of researchers think that high levels of competition have created unkind and aggressive conditions" (Wellcome Trust, 2020, p. 15). This is not very encouraging! However, while you can't control many of the factors that lead to others' competitive behaviours, you can certainly establish your own values around the kind of researcher you want to be and be part of actively resisting the more competitive, negative dynamics within academia. You can also exert agency in considering which research cultures you choose to engage in, across a range of settings (e.g. your department, social media networks, professional associations, and self-formed support groups). Many nurturing, kind, and researcher-centred cultures are out there, and deliberately accessing these environments can enhance your doctoral experience (Ball & Crawford, 2020; Pyhältö et al., 2009).

STUDENT VOICE: "[I benefited from] linking with a broader network of people, especially for activities that promoted focused work or learning (e.g. Shut Up and Write sessions, writing retreats/groups). These opportunities were offered or promoted through the university, and helped by creating a routine where I knew that certain times of the week guaranteed focused work."

It's good to be aware of how to identify healthy and unhealthy research environments. At its foundation, a positive research culture values and encourages research activities, cultivates a sense of belonging, and helps researchers achieve their goals. A positive and healthy research culture enacts things such as shared support for each other's work; respect for different points of view and for diverse career and disciplinary pathways; equitable and ethical distribution of resources; and inclusiveness. The better the institutional culture, the more likely that researchers of all career stages and backgrounds will be actively engaged in supporting each other in their research endeavours and openly sharing their expertise and knowledge. In contrast, unhealthy elements of research cultures include hyper-competitiveness among peers; exclusionary hierarchies; and the extremes of toxic behaviour such as stealing colleagues' ideas, bullying, harassment, or actively devaluing others' work.

The research culture at your enrolling institution is not something you can easily control. That said, it is entirely possible to familiarise yourself with the elements of that culture, get to know what enables (or hinders) your work as a doctoral researcher, and do things that align with your priorities and values. For example, you might find some "kindred spirits" in other doctoral students or staff who are encouraging, energising, and generous; you could foster ongoing interactions with these folks even if the wider department or institutional culture seems to exclude or devalue doctoral researchers as "just students".

STUDENT VOICE: "[Moving to distance study due to the pandemic] pushed me outside of my department, which is relatively small and doesn't have the intellectual or topic support I need to be successful. It allowed me to stop wasting my time in water cooler conversations with people I didn't like but was in close proximity to, and allowed me the time to connect virtually with people I did want to talk to."

Research culture is important because human beings are social creatures. We rely on each other to meet our needs for care and the sense that we belong, and this applies to the academic community we have joined by becoming doctoral students. Recognising research as a social process means understanding that "becoming a researcher does not happen in social isolation" (Mantai, 2017, p. 636). Off-campus doctoral researchers sometimes struggle to feel supported and connected into rich networks that feed their learning, identity, and wellbeing (Erichsen et al., 2014; Kumar et al., 2013). If we become isolated, we can get stuck in unhealthy mindsets or behaviours — and this is why it's so important for each of us to become integrated into a wider researcher community.

In many instances, your access to and engagement with research culture and community depends on *both* the quality of the existing culture itself *and* a certain amount of proactiveness from you in seeking it out. Most often, research culture can't be given to you. It is something which you need to discern and participate in before it feels like it can be "yours". Through reflecting on what's good or challenging within the cultures and communities you encounter, you'll start forming a clearer idea of what you think research communities are about and what it means to be a supportive and supported colleague. Many doctoral researchers take active steps to create better research cultures around them and inspire their peers to do the same.

> **STUDENT VOICE:** "[A highlight from my distance doctoral journey has been] meeting people online from all over the world to read with, write with, create with, make friends with. They have been my rock."

A crucial part of making the most of any research culture is your ability to recognise and show up for opportunities. Your department may have an excellent research culture and offer lots of initiatives for its researchers, but if you don't take up any of the opportunities (e.g. reading your emails to spot opportunities, joining a Zoom seminar, attending a drop-in event, or signing up to help organise a departmental activity), then the benefits of being part of a research culture won't be apparent to you, and it will be more difficult to feel like you're a part of that community. If some of the opportunities available feel exclusionary because of timing or accessibility issues, you could help address this for both yourself and others by requesting a different time or mode of engagement.

Accessing research culture and communities

Research culture and community can be found in many contexts. They exist within your institution and how the institution relates to you, but also in the broader disciplinary and collegial networks that you encounter in both physical and digital communities. While access to technology and the internet may not always be easy in all contexts, many researchers find that engaging actively in digital spaces can be very rewarding and useful for enhancing their access to positive elements of research culture. For those with limited digital connectivity, even an ongoing text or messenger chat or a monthly in-person coffee with one or more fellow doctoral students can make a big difference to disrupting your sense of isolation.

Engaging with digital spaces is powerful for growing academic networks, sustaining a sense of community and belonging, and positioning yourself strongly for career success. Digital communities can be especially important for distance doctoral students, fostering external connections, peer support, and collegial sharing and learning. They also offer an opportunity to deliberately define your professional identity, requiring you to think about how you present yourself, your work, and your research practices. This can be a useful and ongoing process of developing your academic identity and reflecting on how you build your scholarly reputation.

> **STUDENT VOICE:** "A big positive of studying via distance was that I felt the need to join Twitter and [as] a result found a thriving academic community."

There are many kinds of activities that can enhance your experience as a doctoral researcher. This section provides examples of the kinds of initiatives that have proven effective in generating constructive connections for doctoral researchers and their research communities. Some might already be part of your institutional landscape, so the first thing you need to do is check whether something already exists—if so, get involved with that rather than replicating the effort!

Many of the examples below can be led by either doctoral researchers or academic staff. They involve little or no cost and do not need much resourcing to get started. This means you don't have to wait for someone else to make these things happen but can create these opportunities for yourself and your colleagues (we discuss the pros and cons of advocacy and self-organising later in this chapter).

> **STUDENT VOICE:** "If there's no online group, set one up! The vast majority of doctoral students are working at least part of the time remotely. And they are looking for ways to connect; if everyone is not 'in' at the same time, that will have to be online."

Usually, activities such as those outlined below exist within an ecosystem of research endeavours and attitudes, and there are always ways to make them stronger and healthier. All of them could be offered online, in-person, or in hybrid modes, and many could have asynchronous aspects (e.g. associated chats or comments on recordings, ongoing conversations through a platform like Microsoft Teams or Slack) allowing a broad range of researchers to participate.

Communities of research practice and special interest groups

Communities of practice or special interest groups give opportunities for researchers to gather and share knowledge and perspectives, whether across a single discipline, a whole university, or the internet. Creating or participating in such a group is an extremely effective way of building your networks and peer connections, as well as getting your work done within a friendly community context! Below, we introduce examples of these groups and how they work. These are all initiatives that can be run and accessed by doctoral researchers no matter what their location.

Shut Up and Write (SUAW) sessions, which started as a fiction writers' initiative, have now become common in academic settings. These sessions support researchers to get their core work done in an effective and sustainable way. SUAW sessions can vary in length from an hour to a whole day. They often use a time-boxing method called the *pomodoro technique*, developed by Francesco Cirillo when he was a university student in the late 1980s and struggling to focus (sound familiar?). Aside from being effective for meeting your writing goals, additional benefits of SUAW sessions include the consistency of bringing people together in a mutually supportive atmosphere (McChesney, 2017). For more about SUAW sessions, check out *Shut up and write! Some surprising uses of cafés and crowds in doctoral writing* (Mewburn et al., 2014).

> **STUDENT VOICE:** "Shut up and write sessions were ESSENTIAL to my completion."

Writing retreats offer another way of developing research culture and support networks through writing together. A writing retreat is an extended period of time that's dedicated to focusing on your writing goal(s). It requires you to set aside everyday distractions and commitments and devote yourself to writing. This is why writing retreats can often entail a physical relocation to signal a break with normal routines. While enabling your writing goals and allowing you to prioritise your research, the extended time together with your retreat colleagues can also afford opportunities for sharing perspectives, knowledge, and practice around writing and other academic or life issues. Retreats, whether in person or online, often take up a significant amount of time (sometimes including travel as well as the actual writing time), so it's good to know about them early so you can block time out. Disabled folks may want to check out the accessibility of retreat environments and request any accommodations (e.g. a ground floor room) ahead of time to ensure a positive experience. For more information on writing retreats, check out *Academic Writing Retreats: A Facilitators Guide* (Grant, 2008) or examples in the book *Writing*

Groups for Doctoral Education and Beyond (Aitchison & Guerin, 2014).

Reading groups bring together colleagues who are interested in particular topic areas or methods. Several distance doctoral students in our survey mentioned participating in online reading groups. Many reading groups are *discipline- or methodology-based*, perhaps focusing (for example) on autoethnographic research, feminist history, data ethics, clinical trial approaches, or particular methodologies and theories. Others may be *career-based*, focusing on topics like academic writing, research impact, or careers. Reading group members usually take turns selecting and discussing a text that would be of interest to the group. The benefits of these groups extend beyond reading and understanding the texts used—the regular connection with colleagues while prioritising research conversations and perspectives also helps to build collegiality and a learning community. Keynes and Vanderbyl's (2018) journal reading group, which used a "read aloud, think aloud methodology", found that:

> By creating a recurring space of collaboration beyond a visit to the cafe or pub, we've been able to forge an enduring sense of disciplinary and collegial identity via the thrill of engaging genuinely and collaboratively with a piece of writing. (para. 16)

For offer another lovely example of the rich pleasures that can be found in reading (and thinking) together, see Peseta et al. (2019).

Pitching or presentation groups support researchers to develop the key skill of presenting research. Such groups reflect many of the aspects of writing and reading groups mentioned already, but the focus is on developing your next talk or presentation. Participants get to practice their presentations, receive supportive feedback, and learn from hearing and reflecting on other group members' presentations.

Wider networks and communities

Having regular chances to connect with other researchers and engage in research-related learning can help you grow your profile, knowledge, and researcher identity. Connections with academic colleagues also position you well when it comes to hearing about jobs, scholarships, conferences and other events, and publication opportunities in your field. Below are some ways you can nurture your own support networks and access learning opportunities that complement the more structured activities described above.

> **STUDENT VOICE:** "Being amongst peers who are going through the same struggles as you [is] an immensely important part of feeling connected to the academic community."

In-person opportunities to connect with other researchers can still be found or created, even as a distance student! You might be able to find fellow researchers in your local area through community noticeboards, attending local events, or online discussion and support groups. Members of the Women in Academia Support Network (WIASN) on Facebook, for example, sometimes organise meet-ups for those who live in particular locations or to bring together those members who are attending a particular in-person conference. Connecting with other researchers nearby can help launch supportive, congenial relationships. For example, Katrina made it through the final year of her PhD thanks to meeting some other distance doctoral students (all from her home city) at a conference and deciding to meet as an informal, monthly coffee group.

Online networks can also connect you to a wider community of doctoral students and scholars. Some such networks centre on particular disciplines or methodologies while others are for particular groups of people (e.g. women; parents; indigenous scholars; or first-generation doctoral students). We even run a group exactly for students like you—check out the *Doctoral Research by Distance* Facebook group. Most such networks are free to join and run by volunteers, so do be kind, respectful, and realistic in terms of what you expect of the group administrators. These groups also vary in terms of activity and engagement levels, so you may need to try a few before finding networks that work for you. Take care to check the privacy settings of any groups you join (how are new members screened before being admitted? Can those outside the group see who belongs or what they post? Are group members permitted to share group content outside the group environment?) so that you can engage and protect yourself appropriately.

Scholarly associations or societies are a great way to meet more people in your field and find additional research activities that may suit your circumstances. Try asking your supervisor(s) which such groups they are members of or recommend. You could start by attending a conference or symposium run by the association/society, or you could register as a member. Membership often adds you to a mailing list sharing useful information, opportunities, events, and publications. Members may also be able to apply for bursaries, grants, and awards offered by the organisation. Such membership may require paying a fee. However, such fees are often discounted for doctoral researchers, and there can be funding support or waivers for doctoral students—check this both with your institution and the organisation you're interested in joining. And if you're really keen, you could join a scholarly organisation's committee—certainly a fast-track way to get to know, and be known by, colleagues across your field, as well as to contribute to developing research culture.

Partnership agreements are commonly established between universities so that their researchers (including doctoral researchers) have entry and sometimes even borrowing rights at other institutions. Thus, you might be located far from the university where you're enrolled, but thanks to a partnership agreement there may be a university in your local area where you can use the library, attend development workshops and research seminars, or even just hang out in the campus cafe and get a feel for the university campus rhythm. Contact your enrolling institution's international office to see what agreements are in place in your location.

Research events

In almost all academic settings there will be a range of events that bring scholars together to share their work and/or to hear the work of others. Such events are valuable for staying up to date with new work, for being a visible part of your institutional or disciplinary community, for building networks, and for sharing your own work and thus developing your own scholarly identity (see Chapter 5).

Seminars and seminar series are common occurrences in most university departments, with invited speakers presenting to staff and students about their research. Some speakers will likely be graduate students or staff from within the institution, and other guest speakers may come from outside. Seminars are often a good indicator of a group's research health: poor attendance or non-existent seminars can indicate some disengagement and disinterest in the research of others, but sessions that are lively, interesting, and involve active engagement can indicate a level of mutual interest in research topics, openness to discussion and learning, and general collegial goodwill. While you may not be presenting at these in early stages of your doctorate, attending (including online) is an excellent way to get to know the context and culture of your department or faculty. Who is getting invited to speak? Who tends to ask questions, and what are the responses like? How do colleagues chair a session? What kinds of areas are featured in the talks? How many people turn up to the talks? In time, look for opportunities to present your own work in these departmental or institutional events as a stepping stone to presenting at larger events (below).

STUDENT VOICE: "Try and be an active member of your institution, whether that be by attending online seminars or "check ins"—these small connections make all the difference."

Conferences and symposia are part and parcel of knowledge dissemination within academic communities. These events bring together scholars from a range of settings, and some are seen as very prestigious. Alongside attending sessions to hear and discussing the work that's being shared, there are valuable opportunities to participate in social events and informal streams (e.g. online livechats and breakout rooms) to develop stronger connections. Traditionally, academic conferences and symposia have highlighted or perpetuated inequalities, with distance doctoral researchers, early career academics, those with disabilities or caring responsibilities, and those with lesser financial resources facing greater challenges in accessing these events (Burford & Henderson, 2023). Increasingly, however, research workshops and conferences are being held online or in hybrid form, reducing the financial costs, logistical challenges, and climate implications associated with travelling to attend such events. Synchronous and asynchronous approaches have also emerged that can accommodate different time zones and modes of engagement. These changes make disciplinary networks and research culture more accessible to distance doctoral researchers, effectively "moving ideas without moving people" (Chow-Fraser et al, 2018, p. 1). Presenting your own research at some conferences and symposia fuels your developing scholarly identity (see Chapter 5), so consult with your supervisor(s) on opportunities and possible funding for attending these events, and plan ahead for appropriate conferences where you could share your emerging contributions to the field. When you do go, be aware that conferences can be intense, with long days of sessions often followed by social or networking events. Many attendees are deliberately selective about what sessions they attend and how they build in breaks to recharge or build networks. To learn more about the world of conferences, check out *Making Sense of Academic Conferences* (Burford & Henderson, 2023) or the Conference Inference Blog (see https://conferencein ference.wordpress.com/2017/01/30/first-blog-post/).

STUDENT VOICE: "I've had opportunities to attend big-name conferences in my field in many countries, because of the Zoomification of the conference world. This, however, has been a double-edged sword, as there is so much on offer and the Zoom experience is exhausting."

Belonging and accountability

Friendships, networks, and scholarly connections with other researchers are crucial, because it is in relationship with others that we learn how to do research and how to become scholars. Connections you forge in your doctoral studies may become valued friends and collaborators once you are out the other side, or the people you "grow up" alongside if you choose to pursue an academic career. And in a more immediate sense, gathering your people around you supports your wellbeing as well as giving you positive sources of motivation and accountability.

Social/support-focused groups focus primarily on social connections and support for researchers. You might find communities (in your local area or online) for doctoral researchers generally, or for specific groups such as those studying via distance, parents and others with caring responsibilities, those living with chronic illnesses or disabilities, neurodivergent doctoral researchers, or those identifying with queer and transgender communities. The ways these groups may operate can differ greatly, including across in-person, online, synchronous, and asynchronous modes. However, these groups will have in common the purposes of supporting each other and providing encouragement and shared knowledge around issues and challenges that members may be facing. For examples, see Pickard-Smith et al. (2023) and The PhD Pod (2021).

Mastermind, accountability, or peer-learning groups are small groups of peers—usually about three to four people—who meet regularly and informally (in person or online) to share challenges and achievements relevant to their professional life within a solutions-focused framing. Members often come from different disciplines or departments, making such groups a good way to gain institutional and/or academic literacy alongside a welcome dose of collegial support! An important element in creating or joining a group like this is that members must develop trust with each other so that you can share vulnerabilities and difficulties. Such groups are not about getting together to present a "successful" face to each other; they're about honest sharing of both successes and setbacks, with collegial problem-solving, care, and insight.

STUDENT VOICE: "Being online has given me access to researchers from other disciplines which is so good for intellectual stimulation and other perspectives."

Pros and cons of advocacy and self-organising

If you don't have ready access to a healthy research culture, there are ways to create, advocate for, or collaborate on activities that can change this. You can start making things happen around you, and your activities can build momentum or be supported by the local structures of your department or university. Many institutional groups have positions for doctoral representatives on their committees and boards, which may be opportunities worth seeking out if you're passionate about giving doctoral researchers— especially distance doctorates—a voice.

> **STUDENT VOICES:** "I was the Education postgraduate representative which helped me engage with other colleagues about the University and learn about the research process."

Self-organising and banding together with peers to generate stronger research culture can be rewarding on personal and academic community levels. Initiating and participating in these activities supports your development across many areas, including communication and events planning, fundraising, negotiating with a range of university units, and collaboration. It can feel satisfying to make things happen with like-minded others, and to be part of initiatives that encourage and support other researchers like yourself.

There are, however, some negative aspects to watch out for. Excessive time investment is probably the main issue with heavy involvement in organising new initiatives. As long as the time spent feels like it has value for you and supports you in some way towards your own research goals, it's all good. It becomes problematic when these activities take over your schedule or push out time that you would otherwise spend on progressing your research. This can happen occasionally without being a problem; however, when it becomes a consistent pattern, it may need to be addressed.

Another thing to be careful of is getting waylaid by the politics. Being involved in advocacy and self-organising work could mean that you're more likely to encounter organisational politics or come into conflict with others at the institution. It's useful to think about whether any conflict or disagreement that arises is constructive or merely time-consuming and distracting. For example, if you're advocating for the inclusion of doctoral researchers to departmental activities and events, discussing the issue with senior departmental leaders and other academic staff may benefit everyone who is a part of the conversation. However, it's often a fine balance between investing in these forms of academic activism and maintaining good progress on your important doctoral work.

We discuss these considerations not to dissuade you from participating in, creating, or joining a range of events and groups—in fact, we'd strongly encourage these activities—but to flag that there are challenging issues and investments of time that can come with advocacy and self-organising. You may well decide that the potential benefits outweigh any drawbacks, or set limits for yourself on how long and to what extent you'll be involved. Whatever strategy you employ, it's important to keep an eye on your ability to make progress on your doctoral work as well as the downtime and other social time that are essential for overall researcher wellbeing.

Other ways to access researcher development at a distance

The activities and communities we've described in this chapter can support your ongoing development as a scholar. There are also some additional avenues for your research learning that warrant a mention. No doctoral student should be solely reliant on their supervisor(s) for their learning and development. Part of becoming an independent scholar is becoming someone who is able to access a broad platform of learning resources and opportunities.

Digital resources are a rich platform for "feeding" your scholarly self. Wherever you are, you can learn from and be encouraged by podcasts, books, vlogs, and blog posts. These could be about your specific research topic or context, effective research strategies, or the challenges of knowledge work. Through digital resources, you can learn from a wide range of outstanding mentors and hear other doctoral researchers' personal experiences. Embedding this practice in your life—perhaps while you're driving, exercising, or even in the shower!—helps you keep connected around your scholarly interests, extend your knowledge and skills, and cultivate a richer understanding of where and how your work fits into the world.

Advice literature refers to books and resources like this one—things that are specifically written to help you on your academic journey. Advice literature differs from scholarly textbooks that teach you empirical skills or introduce you to theory; advice literature talks explicitly about what doing research can be like, what you might need to learn, and how you might go about navigating this complex journey. Many students aren't even aware that this literature exists, so by having come across this book, you're already ahead of the pack! We've noted some of our favourite advice literature under "Useful resources" at the end of this book. Your university librarian will likely also be able to help you find resources in this genre.

Other opportunities to develop as a researcher come from engaging in research translation activities—that is, re-presenting your research work for wider audiences (such as the public, practitioners in your field, or the media) and on diverse platforms (such as blog posts, videos, and podcasts). You can hone these skills by participating in events such as the "Three Minute Thesis" competitions, attending workshops at your institution or at scholarly conferences, or engaging with the resources provided by external organisations that support research translation. Engaging effectively with broad audiences around your research is a great skill to develop, whether you stay in academia or not.

Ultimately, as a researcher you need a positive research culture, varied learning opportunities, and strong peer support networks around you. We hope the ideas in this chapter give you a sense of hope and agency as well as a range of ideas to draw on. There are always ways in which you can shape your experience and increase your access to research cultures, learning opportunities, and communities, with benefits for your research progress, scholarly identity, and wellbeing.

Activity: Mapping your research ecosystem

Draw a diagram that maps your research "ecosystem". You might use a spider-type diagram to draw lines connecting you with key individuals, groups, or services; you might use a set of concentric circles (with yourself right in the middle) to show how closely you're connected with different elements of research culture and communities. If you're more creatively inclined, you might draw things that symbolise how you feel in relation to research culture; what "feeds" you as a researcher or shapes your sense of belonging and your researcher identity; and where you sense areas of imbalance, learning need, over-reliance, or curiosity.

Then reflect: What does your diagram show you? Are there areas you would benefit from strengthening, or opportunities you think you should consider taking up? Have you engaged in giving as well as taking within the researcher ecosystem? Where might there be opportunities for you to contribute to shaping positive research cultures and communities for both yourself and others?

References

Aitchison, C., & Guerin, C. (Eds.) (2014). *Writing groups for doctoral education and beyond: Innovations in practice and theory.* Routledge.

Ball, K., & Crawford, D. (2020). How to grow a successful—and happy—research team. *International Journal of Behavioral Nutrition and Physical Activity*, *17*(4), 1–3. https://doi.org/10.1186/s12 966-019-0907-1

Burford, J., & Henderson, E. (2023). *Making sense of academic conferences: Presenting, participating and organising.* Routledge.

Chow-Fraser, T., Miya, C., & Rossier, O. (2018). *Moving ideas without moving people: How to e-conference at the University of Alberta.* www.ualberta.ca/kule-institute/media-library/econferencing/e-confe rencing-toolkit-2018-04-10.pdf

Erichsen, E. A., Bolliger, D. U., & Halupa, C. (2014). Student satisfaction with graduate supervision in doctoral programs primarily delivered in distance education settings. *Studies in Higher Education*, *39*(2), 321–338. https://doi.org/10.1080/03075079.2012.709496

Grant, B. (2008). *Academic writing retreats: A facilitators guide.* HERDSA.

Keynes, M., & Vanderbyl, N. (2018). The surprising benefits of a read-aloud reading group [blog post]. Research Whisperer. 24 April, 2018. https://researchwhisperer.org/2018/04/24/the-surprising-benefits-of-a-read-aloud-reading-group/

Kumar, S., Johnson, M., & Hardemon, T. (2013). Dissertations at a distance: Students' perceptions of online mentoring in a doctoral program. *Journal of Distance Education*, *27*(1), 1–11.

Mantai, L. (2017). Feeling like a researcher: Experiences of early doctoral students in Australia. *Studies in Higher Education*, *42*(4), 636–650. https://doi.org/10.1080/03075079.2015.1067603

McChesney, K. (2017, November 13). Survival and solidarity: Virtual shut up and write, parents' edition [blog post]. *Doctoral Writing SIG.*

https://doctoralwriting.wordpress.com/2017/11/13/survival-and-sol idarity-virtual-shut-up-and-write-parents-edition/

Mewburn, I., Osborne, L., & Caldwell, G. (2014). Shut up and write! Some surprising uses of cafes and crowds in doctoral writing. In Guerin, C. & Aitchison, C. (Eds.). *Writing groups for doctoral education and beyond: Innovations in theory and practice* (pp. 399–425). Routledge.

Peseta, T., Fyffe, J., & Sainsbury, F. (2019). Interrogating the "idea of the university" through the pleasures of reading together. In Manathunga, C. & Bottrell, D. (Eds.). *Resisting neoliberalism in higher education, Volume II, Prising open the cracks* (pp. 199–217). https://doi.org/ 10.1007/978-3-319-95834-7_10

Pickard-Smith, K., Belfiore, E., & Bonsall, A. (2023). Feminist online communities: The story of the Women in Academia Support Network— A tale of resistance and online activism. In Ronksley-Pavia, M., Neumann, M. M., Manakil, J., & Pickard-Smith, K. (Eds.). *Academic women: Voicing narratives of gendered experiences* (pp. 161–174). Bloomsbury.

Pyhältö, K., Stubb, J., & Lonka, K. (2009). Developing scholarly communities as learning environments for doctoral students. *International Journal for Academic Development, 14*(3), 221–232. https://doi.org/ 10.1080/13601440903106551

The PhD Pod. (2021, March 16). Pandemic PhDs: Starting a doctorate in 2020. *RED Alert.* http://redalert.blogs.latrobe.edu.au/2021/03/pande mic-phds-starting-doctorate-in.html

Wellcome Trust. (2020). *What researchers think about the culture they work in.* https://cms.wellcome.org/sites/default/files/what-research ers-think-about-the-culture-they-work-in.pdf

8 Unexpected work

Coping with changes and challenges on the distance journey

Over the duration of a doctorate, you are likely to be encounter unexpected changes and challenges as your research unfolds and life happens to you, your supervisor(s), and those you care about. It's very normal to encounter peaks, troughs, and unexpected twists along your journey, so it's a good idea to learn about navigating the unexpected. Therefore, this chapter covers: (i) attitudes toward change in relation to the doctorate; (ii) core strategies to build resilience and ensure you are prepared for the unexpected; (iii) specific strategies for dealing with personal, professional, and study-related changes as a distance doctoral student; (iv) returning and rebuilding after crises and breaks; and (v) the change at the end of the doctorate.

Change is normal in the doctoral journey

Many distance doctoral researchers are confronted with a variety of changes and challenges. Some may be planned or things you've chosen; others may be unplanned and beyond your control. Some may affect everyone at your

DOI: 10.4324/9781003334088-8

institution, workplace, or community, while some may affect only you. Many changes will influence more than one aspect of your life; for example, embarking on a doctorate full-time (a study-related change) is likely to lead to a reduction or pausing of paid work (a professional change), with an associated drop in household income (personal change). And it's not only your circumstances that might evolve—as we explored in Chapter 5, a doctorate also brings changes *inside you* as you transform from a student to a researcher, wrestling with feelings of liminality or "between-ness" and the uncertainty of moving from the known into the unknown realm of original research (Jazvac-Martek et al., 2011).

The changes and challenges we face can impact our wellbeing, progress, and outcomes, but the impacts are mediated by the specific ways we choose to respond (Brenner 2019). It's important to recognise that change is not necessarily a bad thing. We might be energised or liberated when our circumstances or relationships change; we might choose to make changes as we deliberately shape the life we want; or we might gain some of life's greatest gifts as our families grow or as we take life-changing steps in response to unexpected opportunities. Experiences of coping with changes and challenges also build our resilience, self-understanding, and independence, helping us lead more balanced and empowered lives.

While we can't foresee the specific things that lie ahead of us, we can anticipate that there may well be *some form(s) of* change and/or challenge on the journey ahead. In our 2022 survey, we asked over 500 distance doctoral students to identify all the major life events that had happened during their doctoral enrolment. Only a quarter reported none; the others reported up to *seventeen* major life events within the years of their doctorates! The average number of major life events our participants reported was 3.84—and this data doesn't include any changes or challenges associated with the doctorate itself (e.g. changes of supervisor, failed experiments, or struggling with the cognitive and creative demands of producing a compelling original contribution to knowledge). We think it's clear that the best plan is to expect the unexpected, rather than anticipating a perfect ride!

Armed with this knowledge, you can proactively grow your ability to deal with change, become aware of the possible challenges that might arise, and develop strategies that can help you deal with adversity (Brenner 2019; Degtyareva 2020). These actions can help you navigate whatever changes or "bumps in the road" may emerge. Let's get into it!

Strategies for all seasons

While we can't account for every situation that you may encounter, there are core strategies that will support you in the good times and also equip you with knowledge, support systems, and resilience for when changes and challenges arise. Arguably, the thing that's most important across the board is to *be proactive*. This can manifest in a multitude of ways that equip you with knowledge and support networks and enable you to access help and respond wisely when challenges arise. The distance doctoral students who responded to our survey had lots to say here:

- "Be proactive about getting to know people."
- "Be proactive about self care."

- "Be proactive in developing support networks."
- "Be proactive. Seek help if you are flailing; ask a fellow student if you don't want to or can't access help via formal channels. If you need mental health support, ask for it."
- "Be proactive in seeking and connecting with learning resources."
- "Be proactive in organising meetings with colleagues/ supervisors."
- "Be proactive at seeking out support when you need it."
- "Be proactive in contacting people."
- "Be proactive and find your own opportunities."
- "Be proactive and clear with communications."
- "Be proactive in emailing people, catch up when possible."

Building institutional literacy (see Chapter 2) also helps you prepare for potential adverse circumstances. Finding out what support services are on offer and how you can access them from off-campus means you're prepared if you need this support later on. Student union representatives, hardship funds, accessibility services, and academic and wellbeing supports are examples of the provision many universities offer to their students.

Having supportive networks of peers with whom you can discuss issues (see Chapter 7) is crucial when things don't go as you'd hope. However, unless you've invested in establishing your networks in the good times, you may find yourself facing changes and challenges alone. Peer networks can be extremely useful for sounding out possible solutions, offering encouragement or comfort, and connecting you to others who could help.

Remaining "visible" to your supervisor(s) and other colleagues is really important. As a distance doctoral researcher, there is a risk of you being "out of sight, out of mind" for busy supervisors or other university staff, and this can be compounded if you hide yourself away when trouble comes. Maintain regular, open communication, no matter what life throws your way. People can only help and support you if they are aware of what's happening.

The sections that follow explore some of the more specific changes and challenges that may come up during a doctorate. Keep in mind that these are only examples and possibilities. Everyone's situation, and the strategies that are needed in each situation, will be unique.

Strategies for dealing with personal changes and challenges

There are many types of changes in personal circumstances. You may experience family changes like the births of children, changes in close relationships, and/ or increased caring responsibilities. Your physical and/or mental health may change, either for a fixed time or more permanently. You might need to leave your home, family, or country for all or part of your doctoral enrolment or to conduct fieldwork. Severe personal challenges include experiencing housing or food insecurity; having to deal with war, displacement, or a natural disaster; facing acute health challenges; or being the victim of crime, abuse, or another traumatic event. Continuing with your doctoral research at a distance when your basic needs (including food and shelter) are under threat or not being met can be exceedingly difficult (Gordon, 2023).

Personal changes and challenges are often unexpected, but they can influence your wellbeing and research progress significantly (Sverdlik et al., 2018). You might need to temporarily step away from your studies to deal with whatever issues have arisen. If this is relatively brief, negotiate adjusted timelines with your supervisor(s) or other staff. If you need more time to address a more serious situation, consider applying for a temporary suspension of your enrolment. Sometimes students worry that asking for a suspension will reflect badly on them, but these processes exist for exactly this type of reason: to prevent a chunk of your enrolment time being eaten away while your circumstances mean you can't meaningfully progress your doctoral work.

> **STUDENT VOICE:** "It's ok to take a break—maybe an interruption of study if it gets a bit much."

Personal challenges often prompt you to review your circumstances—especially if you want to continue making progress with your studies in difficult times. The strategies in Chapters 3 and 4 can help you set healthy boundaries, negotiate carefully and clearly with those around you, and identify when and how you will continue to work on your research. If necessary, reach out to a coach or counsellor for support in doing this thinking or rehearsing difficult conversations. If it's available and/or affordable, additional practical support (such as childcare, cleaning/housework assistance, or outsourcing tasks such as transcription) can also relieve some of the pressure at these times.

Serious personal changes and challenges such as physical or psychological health-related issues and trauma require professional attention and support, as we noted in Chapter 5. Seek help as soon as possible from a qualified health professional. If you alert them to your study goals and demands, they can likely help you think through a safe, healthy, and realistic way forward in your situation. Documentation from these professionals can also help you apply for special accommodations, a study extension, or a temporary suspension.

> **STUDENT VOICE:** "I experienced burnout, to the point where I considered dropping out of the PhD programme. While this was difficult, it helped break down my unrealistic expectations of myself and others, and forced me to face up to the ways I have relied on extrinsic motivation to get work done in ways that were unsustainable."

And where's your supervisor in all this? It's a tricky balance: Your personal circumstances fall outside your supervisor's control or responsibility, yet will almost certainly affect your research progress. It remains your choice whether to share sensitive information, but given that your supervisors are invested in your study (and have their own personal and professional lives to plan), we recommend you at least inform them if you are experiencing changes and challenges that affect your progress. Although your supervisor(s) can (and should) show empathy and compassion, intervening in your personal affairs falls outside of responsible supervisory practice. Instead, they may be able to refer you to available support services, help you apply for an extension or temporary suspension of your studies, adjust timelines and plans, and/or negotiate extensions with funders. But remember, supervisors can only intervene and support you in these ways if they are made aware of your circumstances. Whatever you do, don't just disappear and cease communicating with your supervisor(s). This will only make it more difficult for them to support you.

Finally, keep in mind that your institutional support team (including peers, mentors, support staff and supervisors) may not always know what your family circumstances or cultural and/or religious norms demand of you. Sharing the impact that these have on your research life can help cultivate mutual understanding and respect, both in the good times and when changes and challenges arise.

Strategies for dealing with professional changes and challenges

Changes in professional circumstances include changes in your employment status (e.g. part-time to full-time; fixed-term contracts), promotions, redundancies, job role changes, or even a shift into a new career. Such changes can have flow-on effects to your financial situation, your time, where you live, or your levels of short-term or ongoing stress. Professional changes and challenges can also influence your ability to focus on your study and may require you to adapt your mode of study (on-campus vs distance; part-time vs full-time enrolment) or engage differently with institutional processes and structures.

As elsewhere, open and proactive communication is important. Make sure relevant colleagues are aware of the demands of your doctoral studies, and check into the possible support or accommodations your employer might offer such as flexible hours or a contribution to your study costs. If your employer is supporting your study financially, keep on top of administrative processes such as support letters from your supervisor, progress reports, and billing/fee payment.

> **STUDENT VOICE:** "[Something that helped me was] working compressed hours at my day job so there was one designated weekday for my PhD work. This was discussed and agreed with my line manager well before I started the PhD. The approach was adopted from other staff who had undertaken the same process or were working compressed hours for other purposes (e.g. childcare). This has allowed me time to focus on the PhD during the week."

Perhaps you have access to study or refreshment leave through your employment—when might this leave benefit your study progress the most? To maintain good-will, talk with your employer about study leave timing well in advance so your role can be covered appropriately. Or perhaps you've taken time out from your job while completing your studies. If so, try to plan timelines carefully to avoid clashing overlaps when you return to work. Keeping abreast of what is happening in your workplace and what will be expected on your return may help smooth your transition back to work, or it may just add to your stress levels and distraction while you're trying to focus on your doctorate. Give yourself permission to do what feels right for you.

Uncertainty around contracts, job changes, and working hours are normal considerations for many workers. It may be wise to try to build your savings before starting your doctorate to create a buffer for any unexpected job changes that affect your income; this is especially important if you're a self-funded doctoral student. If you find yourself needing to seek a new job during your doctorate, reach out to your university's employment/ careers unit. These teams can assist with job-seeking efforts (such as curriculum vitae and interview preparation) and industry networking opportunities; some also offer workshops, courses, or internship opportunities. Ask how you can make use of these services from off-campus, and consider if there are any in-person opportunities you particularly want to attend.

> **STUDENT VOICE:** "COVID-19 meant a big increase in workload in my day job, which made it much harder to fit in research and professional development."

Strategies for dealing with study changes and challenges

Very few doctoral studies proceed exactly as planned! Common challenges related to doctoral projects include issues with finding relevant and recent literature, delays in ethical and/or institutional permission clearances, failed experiments or fieldwork exercises, difficulties finding or retaining participants, struggling to understand supervisors' feedback, delays in receiving supervisor feedback, unexpected changes or unavailability of supervisors, rejections of work submitted to academic journals or conferences, or milestones or progress reviews that are less than satisfactory.

Understanding that these research-related challenges are common (and in some cases may have no relation to your actual ability) is an important first step in working through them. You are not the first and won't be the last to encounter tricky research-related issues! It is how you deal with these issues that will determine your success. Open communication with your supervisors and with your support networks and peers is important (as always!), as is using your initiative and taking responsibility for leading your own learning—it's not your supervisors' job to show you how to do everything or resolve all the tricky parts of the project for you (see Chapter 6). Make use of the supports available at your institution (see Chapter 2) and more widely (see Chapter 7), and just keep going. You are meant to keep walking forward through the challenges that your particular project throws up, and you will learn and grow as a result.

> **STUDENT VOICE:** "State border restrictions made me miss a lot of fieldwork opportunities (approx. 1 year), resulting in me missing important data collection and collaborative networking opportunities. I was devastated for a long time. I overcame this by developing review chapters that did not require fieldwork, and did my best to maintain contact with my collaborators through Zoom meetings."

Other study-related things to consider include moving between part-time and full-time study, moving between on-campus and distance study, and changing supervisors. These changes may or may not be your choices; many doctoral researchers, for example, became distance students unexpectedly when the COVID-19 pandemic sent communities and countries into lockdown (Jackman et al., 2022).

Changes in your mode of study or supervisory arrangements are usually governed by university policies and procedures. Information about these should be available via phone/email from your programme administrators or graduate school and/or located on your institution's website. Your supervisors will also likely have had past students go through the process of changing study modes or supervisors and may be able to point you in the right direction, although do be mindful that processes change and supervisors' information may not be the most up to date. It's a good idea to discuss possible changes to study modes with your supervisors before completing the paperwork, both as a courtesy and because their experience may inform your decision.

Changes to supervisory panels are more frequent than you might imagine. Reasons can include supervisors changing jobs or retiring, addressing a supervisor's workload, or even a supervisor passing away (Wisker & Robinson, 2013). The most common reason, however, is issues within the supervisory relationship (Schmidt & Hansson, 2022). If you are struggling with your supervisory relationship, start by reviewing the advice in Chapter 6. There may be small things you can do to try and nurture more positive relationships and/or more productive ways of working and communicating. Milestones such as progress reports also offer natural opportunities to have a friendly check-in around what's working well for each party and where expectations may be out of alignment. Getting perspective from other doctoral students in your networks can be helpful in calibrating your expectations. However, be aware that this is subjective information, and be sure to also seek out your institution's policies around supervision expectations.

If you don't think you're going to be able to proceed, produce a satisfactory thesis or dissertation, and remain healthy and well while working with your current supervisor(s), it's important to take action. Do not live under the illusion that "things will sort themselves out". Approach your school of graduate research or a senior staff member in your academic department, first to have an informal conversation and then, if necessary, to proceed with requesting a change. It's never nice (for either students or supervisors) to acknowledge that a supervisory relationship is not working, but it may be what's needed for you to progress. In Schmidt and Hansson's

(2022) study, doctoral students who changed supervisors "experienced the long decision-making processes as stressful, difficult and exhausting, sometimes causing a lack of mental well-being. However, once the change was complete, they felt renewed, energized and capable of continuing with their studies" (p. 54).

Returning and rebuilding after crises and breaks

Despite your best efforts, you may find you simply cannot proceed with your studies for some time. It may take longer than you would like to claw back a sense of normality in other areas of your life, and you may find you become increasingly disconnected from even the idea of your doctorate. Some students do choose to walk away in this situation, and it's important to feel a sense of agency here. Giving yourself permission to let the doctorate go might be the wisest and healthiest path. If you do decide to resume your studies, the advice below is for you—but we don't want to suggest that resuming is the only honourable choice. Only you will know what is right for you.

If you've decided to restart your doctorate, take a moment to acknowledge your courage in taking this step. Resuming because you are *choosing to* (rather than because you feel you "should") can make a big difference to your mindset and behaviour. This courage and agency can be harnessed in many other areas, such as in making the first contact with your supervisors (or perhaps new supervisors, if the original team are no longer available) and graduate school. Re-opening these lines of communication early in the process will be critical for ensuring you understand the options available to you and begin to feel connected and supported once again.

If it's been some time since you worked on your project, the study itself may need reviewing. Perhaps you hadn't yet begun your fieldwork, and so you need to return to the literature to see how knowledge has advanced in your area while you've been away. If others have stepped in and filled the gap you were hoping to address, identifying this early can allow you to adapt your study (in consultation with supervisors, and if necessary through a formal institutional approval process for the change of topic) so that you are well-placed to make an original contribution to knowledge. If you do have data and are worried it's getting "cold", rest assured that many scholars publish their findings years after they collected their data. Return to the literature; consider where there are spaces into which your data might allow you to contribute; and sharpen your research questions or analytical lenses to facilitate those purposeful contributions.

While you'll know some things about the doctoral journey from your earlier work, you will have changed and you may be feeling a bit fragile or vulnerable as you take those tentative steps back into academic spaces. Be mindful that returning to your desk, your supervisors, or other doctoral things may trigger a return of some of the worst feelings you were experiencing at the time you had to step away from your studies, even if the doctorate itself wasn't the reason you had to push "pause". Our brains are complex and sometimes connect the wrong things; if you find yourself avoiding your doctorate once you've resumed, consider accessing some counselling or coaching to try and unpack what might be going on and how you might reframe things more productively.

Ultimately, we would encourage you to view your "re-start" as more of a "full start". As you pick up your studies again, we suggest reading through this whole book (and other relevant advice literature, e.g. Brabazon, 2022) to equip yourself with confidence, ideas, and practical strategies in all areas of your doctoral journey. Give yourself permission to try different ways of working, and prioritise putting in place the things that are known to facilitate doctoral students' progress (Chapters 3 and 4), wellbeing (Chapter 5), supervision relationships (Chapter 6), and support networks and learning (Chapter 7).

The change at the end of the doctoral journey

With all the changes and challenges to contend with *during* the course of your doctorate, it's understandable to view completing your doctorate as a gateway to rest and relief. It can certainly be this, but finishing your research can sometimes also leave an uncomfortable "hole" in your life and leave you struggling with the question of "what next?".

After graduation, many new doctors find themselves unemployed despite their acknowledged expertise—a surreal position to be in! Dealing with the transition from doctoral research to job-seeking, or transitioning back into an existing professional role when you have taken some time out to complete your doctorate, can be complex, time-consuming, and challenging (Sverdlik et al., 2018). Some graduates also experience post-PhD sadness or depression. It's good to be aware that this can happen and establish ways to pre-empt or ameliorate it such as planning things to look forward to post-completion (a family holiday after all the "no, I'm working" responses?), remaining active in communities and places that affirm your expertise (such as presenting at conferences), maintaining rather than abandoning your peer networks, and giving yourself permission to experience a wide range of feelings after this draining but exhilarating journey.

As you transition out of your doctoral programme, you will likely lose access to many university facilities. However, alternative arrangements can usually be made for doctoral alumni wishing to remain part of the academic community—perhaps a non-salaried adjunct appointment or an alumni subscription to the library and other institutional resources. Ask your supervisor(s) or academic librarians about options here, and join your alumni network to stay up-to-date on university news and opportunities for future research collaborations and outputs. An ongoing relationship between yourself and the university can be a win-win situation for both sides. Moreover, although you're stepping back from the university itself, you don't have to leave the professional networks or communities you've been involved in. Continue participating in the activities they offer such as conferences, workshops, and short courses, and take advantage of opportunities to present your doctoral work to appropriate academic, industry, and community groups.

To conclude, doing something as ambitious and long-term as a doctorate is going to entail some changes and challenges for any student. However, these unexpected turns can offer opportunities for different kinds of development and growth. Being proactive, well-informed, connected to appropriate supports, and a good communicator can stand distance doctoral students in good stead through the unexpected and out the other side.

Activity: Life grid reflection

Life grids help us visualise the ups and downs of our lives, whether overall or in specific domains. Drawing the "shape" or trajectory of our lives over time helps us see the big picture of our journey and reflect on our experiences. Jackman and Sisson (2022) used this technique with doctoral students, and we think it's a great way for you to "zoom out" and consider your experiences to this point, as well as an appropriate activity as we approach the end of this book. In addition to acknowledging what you've been through and coped with, this exercise also reminds you that ups, downs, and bumps in the road are to be expected—making this reality something we need to bear in mind for our future planning.

Start with a template; you can download an editable version of the template below from our website (www. doctoralresearchbydistance.wordpress.com) or make your own. Set up time markers across the top, in equal increments, beginning at the start of your doctoral journey (this could be the start of your enrolment or even earlier when you first started exploring or preparing for a doctorate). Depending on how far through your doctoral journey you are, you might count off the time across the top of the grid in weeks, months, quarters, semesters, or even years! You may also like to ensure that your template extends into the future (perhaps to the time when you anticipate submitting or graduating); this way, your life grid could become a "living document" that you add to periodically as you continue to track your journey through to completion.

In the rows for your doctoral and personal journeys respectively, write in key events, changes, and challenges that arose in particular time periods. In the row for your sense of wellbeing, draw a continuous, freehand line that "graphs" your wellbeing as it moves on a spectrum from low to high over time. The events in the doctoral and personal journey rows above may have been key factors in influencing shifts in your wellbeing; alternatively, you may have had other strategies and supports in place to protect your wellbeing that meant you were better able to cope with the doctoral and/or personal challenges you encountered.

You can adjust the template to suit yourself. You might like to add rows in which you graph things like your confidence as an emerging scholar; your relationship(s) with your supervisor(s); your emotions and attitude towards your doctoral work; your physical health and wellness; or anything else that you'd like to be able to capture.

Be proud as you look at your completed life grid; acknowledge all that you have encountered and celebrate the fact that you are still here, still pursuing your aspiration of completing a doctorate, and still engaged in the rich and challenging work that this aspiration requires of you. Reflect on what has helped you navigate the various ups, downs, and bumps in the road, and what you might like to put in place to better prepare you for whatever might lie ahead. The ideas in other chapters of this book can help you with this.

Time (in equal-length increments)	e.g. Jan-Mar 2023	e.g. Apr-Jun 2023	e.g. Jul-Sep 2023	...		
Doctoral journey (key milestones & phases)						
Personal journey (key life events & changes)						
Sense of wellbeing HIGH LOW						

References

Brabazon, T. (2022). *Comma: How to restart, reclaim and reboot your PhD*. Author's Republic.

Brenner, A. (2019, 28 September). 7 tips to help you successfully respond to change. *Psychology Today*. www.psychologytoday.com/us/blog/in-flux/201909/7-tips-help-you-successfully-respond-change

Degtyareva, O. (2020, 17 November). When it comes to being productive, it's best to embrace uncertainty. *Research Whisperer*. https://researchwhisperer.org/2020/11/17/when-it-comes-to-being-productive-its-best-to-embrace-uncertainty/

Gordon, K. (2023, 23 March). Crisis and care in PGR education. *The Auditorium*. https://theauditorium.blog/2023/03/23/crisis-and-care-in-pgr-education/

Jackman, P. C., Sanderson, R., Haughey, T. J., Brett, C. E., White, N., Zile, A., Tyrrell, K., & Byrom, N. C. (2022). The impact of the first COVID-19 lockdown in the UK for doctoral and early career researchers. *Higher Education*, *84*, 705–722. https://doi.org/10.1007/s10734-021-00795-4

Jackman, P. C., & Sisson, K. (2022). Promoting psychological well-being in doctoral students: A qualitative study adopting a positive psychology perspective. *Studies in Graduate and Postdoctoral Education*, *13*(1), 19–35. https://doi.org/10.1108/SGPE-11-2020-0073

Jazvac-Martek, M., Chen, S., & McAlpine, L. (2011). Tracking the doctoral student experience over time: Cultivating agency in diverse spaces. In McAlpine, L. & Amundsen, C. (Eds.). *Doctoral education: Research-based strategies for doctoral students, supervisors and administrators* (pp. 17–36). Springer.

Schmidt, M., & Hansson, E. (2022). "I didn't want to be a troublemaker": Doctoral students' experiences of change in supervisory arrangements. *Studies in Graduate and Postdoctoral Education*, *13*(1), 54–73. https://doi.org/10.1108/SGPE-02-2021-0011

Sverdlik, A., Hall, N. C., McAlpine, L., & Hubbard, K. (2018). The PhD experience: A review of the factors influencing doctoral students' completion, achievement, and well-being. *International Journal of Doctoral Studies*, *13*, 361–388. https://doi.org/10.28945/4113

Wisker, G., & Robinson, G. (2013). Doctoral "orphans": Nurturing and supporting the success of postgraduates who have lost their supervisors. *Higher Education Research & Development*, *32*(2), 300–313. https://doi.org/10.1080/07294360.2012.657160

9 Final thoughts

We began this book acknowledging the rich diversity of distance doctoral students and the power and importance of off-campus and hybrid doctoral study modes. As you've read through this book, we hope you've seen yourself and your circumstances, motivations, aspirations, and experiences among the pages. We hope you've gained new understandings of the complexities that accompany doctoral study and how these can be navigated off-campus. We also hope the authentic student voice we've included has inspired and encouraged you, reassuring that you are not alone and that distance modes can indeed be very positive ways to engage in doctoral study.

> **STUDENT VOICE:** "I'm on my way to achieve my dual dream of writing a novel AND procuring a PhD. Along the way, I've had opportunities to work with outstanding scholars and writers in my field. In many ways, being a distance student is helping to prepare me for the life of a creative writer. It has taught me how to independently research and write, yet also be part of a writing and scholarly community. I have had to learn to manage my time, resources and working conditions. It has given me the flexibility to do all of this while also being a functioning family member, businessperson and surviving a worldwide pandemic."

DOI: 10.4324/9781003334088-9

Through this book, we've emphasised that you have agency to shape your own journey within the imperfect and complex landscape of distance doctoral education. There is so much that you can do to take ownership of your journey, managing the inner work of becoming doctoral as well as the outer work and juggling work of managing your time, tasks, and other responsibilities. We hope this book has given you advance warning of both challenges and opportunities, allowing you to proactively make sense of and shape what happens along your journey.

As we argued in Chapter 1, off-campus doctoral research pathways need to be normalised, celebrated, and well supported. This book is part of our contribution to supporting distance doctoral students and raising awareness of this important cohort. While we've written primarily for students, we hope that supervisors, graduate school staff, and higher education policy makers might also be both challenged and equipped by this book. In our workshops with higher education staff around the globe, we've expressed our view that high-quality provision for off-campus doctoral students is both a moral imperative (all students have the right to an equitable educational experience) and a commercial advantage (institutions that support off-campus students well are more likely to recruit and retain such students).

Sometimes, the reason things haven't changed yet is not because of a deep-seated commitment to current practices but rather because nobody has stopped to consider that things could be better or different. So, we encourage you to speak up in your own context. Ask for things that you would find helpful and, to the extent you feel comfortable, challenge your institution to work in ways that respect your situation as an off-campus doctoral student. We don't mean to suggest that you should bear all the responsibility for educating your institution—indeed, in Chapter 2, we advised prospective doctoral researchers to consider seeking a university that already has good provision for off-campus students. However, one of the forms your agency around your doctoral experience might take is you having a voice and speaking back to your supervisor(s), institution, or administrators.

To close, we wish to highlight once again how wonderful distance, off-campus, hybrid, and remote doctoral education pathways can be. We included the word *flourishing* in the title of this book deliberately—we don't want you to just *survive* your distance journey but rather to embrace the possibilities that come from studying off campus. It is time we all moved on from outdated deficit narratives suggesting that distance study was somehow second-best or that it was students' foolish choice to give up the opportunities that on-campus study afforded. In the twenty-first century, as doctoral cohorts are more diverse than ever before, doctoral programmes and pathways must be similarly diverse, and every single doctoral student—no matter their background, context, or circumstances—should feel that they belong, are seen, and are supported on the exciting adventure of becoming doctoral.

STUDENT VOICE: "I graduated!! My proudest success was completing my study while juggling a growing family, working full time, and running a business. Being a distance student meant I could achieve this—as there was no option for me to be on campus where I live. This success happened due to the support I had from my family, and my supervisors, as well as my passion and thorough enjoyment of the learning process and my research topic. I love learning and if I could do it full time all the time I would!"

Activity: Checking in with your present and future self

Websites such as www.futureme.org/ and https://thes elf.club/future-self/ let you enter a letter to your future self, an email address that the letter should be sent to, and the date you'd like the letter sent. When the letter makes its way back to you in weeks, months, or even years to come, reading it will give you food for thought and remind you how far you've travelled over the intervening time.

Using one of these platforms, write a letter to your future self reflecting on some of the prompts below. Schedule it to be returned to you in six months, a year, or whenever you think you might need to check in again with yourself. (Just make sure you use an email address that you expect to still have in the future—not your student email account, if you're approaching graduation!)

- Right now, how would you describe your progress on the journey from "student" to "scholar"?
- What identities are you experiencing or juggling at the moment? How is that feeling?
- What has been helping you in your distance doctoral journey?
- What are you learning about how to inhabit the identities you value and how to live in ways that protect your health and wellbeing?
- What are your goals or aspirations for this next season of your life?
- What might Future (Dr) You need to hear, remember, revisit, or reflect on?

Useful resources

Books

Here are some of our favourite "advice literature" resources. All are titles we have used with the doctoral researchers we support.

Book series:

- All the titles in the *Insider Guides to Success in Academia*[1] book series (published by Routledge). At the time of writing, the series included books on international doctoral students; part-time doctoral students; key milestones in the doctorate (including surviving the final year and the oral defence); writing and publishing; and engaging in research culture and building your research impact.
- The *Wellbeing and Self-care in Higher Education: Embracing Positive Solutions*[2] book series (published by Routledge).
- The *ThinkWell* books[3] and ebooks[4] by Hugh Kearns and Maria Gardiner.

Individual titles (in alphabetical order):

- Ayres, Z. (2022). *Managing your mental health during your PhD: A survival guide*. Springer.
- Boynton, P. (2017). *The research companion*. Routledge.

- Denscombe, M. (2012). *Research proposals: A practical guide*. Open University Press.
- McMaster, C., Frick, L., & Motshoane, P. (Eds.). (2016). *Postgraduate study in South Africa: Surviving and succeeding*. African Sun Media.
- McMaster, C., & Murphy, C. (Eds.). (2014). *Postgraduate study in Aotearoa New Zealand: Surviving and succeeding*. NZCER Press.
- McMaster, C., & Murphy, C. (Eds.). (2016). *Graduate study in the USA: Surviving and succeeding*. Peter Lang.
- McMaster, C., Murphy, C., & de Lasson, J. (Eds.). (2017). *The Nordic PhD: Surviving and succeeding*. Peter Lang.
- McMaster, C., Murphy, C., Whitburn, B., & Mewburn, I. (Eds.). (2017). *Postgraduate study in Australia: Surviving and succeeding*. Peter Lang.
- Mewburn, I. (2020). *How to tame your PhD* (2nd ed.). Lulu Press.
- Mewburn, I., Firth, K., & Lehmann, S. (2018). *How to fix your academic writing trouble*. McGraw Hill.
- Phillips, E., & Pugh, D. (2015). *How to get a PhD: A handbook for students and their supervisors*. McGraw Hill.
- Sheldon, J., & Sheppard, V. (2022). *Online communities for doctoral researchers and their supervisors: Building engagement with social media*. Routledge.
- Thomson, P., & Kamler, P. (2016). *Detox your writing: Strategies for doctoral researchers*. Routledge.

Online communities and resources

Online content evolves at an ever-increasing pace, yet it is a core resource for many doctoral students. We didn't want to omit online resources, but we are aware that anything we recommend might become outdated or cease to exist. Equally, useful new sites will appear over time. We have therefore only included a small selection of the most well-established (at the time of writing) online groups and resources here. Beyond this, we encourage you to reach out to your networks (see Chapter 7) for their recommendations of useful online resources.

Websites and blogs

- Our own website (https://doctoralresearchbydistance. wordpress.com)—resources and support materials specifically aimed at distance doctoral researchers.
- Pat Thompson's *Patter* blog (https://patthomson.net)— researcher development and academic writing.
- Helen Kara's blog (https://helenkara.com/blog/)— researcher development and research methods.
- Inger Mewburn's *The Thesis Whisperer* blog (https:// thesiswhisperer.com)—a variety of resources aimed at supporting doctoral researchers and early career academics.
- The *Conference Inference* blog (https://conferencein ference.wordpress.com/)—understanding the weird world of academic conferences.
- Tara Brabazon (www.youtube.com/@TaraBrabazon Channel/)—a series of 300 Vlogs specifically for doctoral students, plus a wide range of other videos

around higher education, research, supervision, and researcher development.

- The *Neurodiversity Hub* (www.neurodiversityhub.org/resources-for-universities)—a website full of advice, resources, and links for neurodivergent students and those who support them, including university-focused materials

Facebook

- Our *Doctoral Research by Distance* Facebook group (www.facebook.com/groups/doctoralresearchbydistance/)—an interactive, dedicated space for distance doctoral students to meet and share their experiences.
- *PhD and Early Career Researcher Parents* (www.facebook.com/groups/776957585681408)
- *Women in Academia Support Network Careers Support #wiasn* (www.facebook.com/groups/905644729576673)
- *Academic Women Online Writing Retreat* (www.facebook.com/groups/1617153205104240)—a community of women doctoral students and academics who meet online to write in the company of others.
- *Doctoral Mom* (www.facebook.com/groups/306082170038366)

Notes

1 www.routledge.com/Insider-Guides-to-Success-in-Academia/book-series/IGSA
2 www.routledge.com/Wellbeing-and-Self-care-in-Higher-Education/book-series/WSCHE
3 www.ithinkwell.com.au/bookshop
4 www.ithinkwell.com.au/ebooks

Index